WHITE HOUSE KiDS

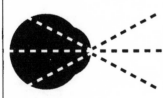

This Large Print Book carries the
Seal of Approval of N.A.V.H.

WHITE HOUSE KiDS

SUSAN EDWARDS

Thorndike Press • Thorndike, Maine

Copyright © 1999 by Bill Adler Books.

Published in 2000 by arrangement with Avon Books, an imprint of HarperCollins Publishers, Inc.

Thorndike Press Large Print Americana Series.

The tree indicium is a trademark of Thorndike Press.

The text of this Large Print edition is unabridged.
Other aspects of the book may vary from the original edition.

Set in 16 pt. Plantin by Susan Guthrie.

Printed in the United States on permanent paper.

Library of Congress Cataloging-in-Publication Data

Edwards, Susan, 1948–
   White House kids / Susan Edwards.
      p. cm.
   ISBN 0-7862-2789-3 (lg. print : hc : alk. paper)
      1. Children of presidents — United States — History.
   2. Children of presidents — United States — Biography.
   3. White House (Washington, D.C.) — History. 4. Large
   type books. I. Title.

E176.45 .E39 2000
973′.09′9—dc21   00-044686

"Nobody likes to leave the White House, whatever they say. We are no exception. There is a photograph of the whole family about to leave and I must say we look as though we are being expelled from the Garden of Eden."

ALICE ROOSEVELT LONGWORTH

Contents

∽

Part I: 1801–1944
THE PRESIDENT'S HOUSE

Part II: 1944–1998
IN THE MEDIA AGE

PART I

～

1801–1944

THE PRESIDENT'S HOUSE

～

1

To Make It a Home

The White House is the seat of government for the executive branch, where political problems are debated until late into the night, congressional bills are signed with a flourish, glittering state dinners for foreign kings, queens, and prime ministers are held, and where, sometimes, the fate of humanity in a nuclear age hangs in the balance. But it has also been the home to forty presidents and their families — forty rather than forty-two because George Washington never got to live in it and Grover Cleveland was both our twenty-second and twenty-fourth president, serving two separated rather than consecutive terms as president. Because it is a home as well as a vast office complex, its walls have reverberated to the sound of children's laughter and temper tantrums, and its every nook and cranny has been explored by youngsters in search of mischief or hiding from parents and nannies. Its roof has been home to young Jesse Grant's telescope and Alice Roosevelt's secret cigarette smoking. The children of several presidents have discovered that the East Room, its grandest public space, makes a terrific roller skating rink. Its grounds have been the site of slides and swings and tree houses, and children from Tad and Willie Lincoln through Archie Roosevelt to Caroline Kennedy have ridden their ponies over the expansive White House lawns. An entire menagerie of pets — not just cats and dogs, but exotic birds, guinea pigs, goats, and ducks — have found a home at the White House at the insistence of generations of White House kids.

This most significant and famous of all American homes has seen great changes in terms of its physical structure over the nearly two hundred years of its existence. The site, like that of the city of Washington itself, was chosen by the first American president, George Washington, who had been a surveyor before he led the colonists to victory in the Revolutionary War. Initial plans for a palatial European-style edifice were abandoned at the insistence of Thomas Jefferson, and the Irish-born architect James Hoban won a contest to provide a new design. Our second president, John Adams, moved into the still unfinished building in 1800; Abigail Adams hung the family laundry to dry in the unplastered East Room.

The building was originally called the Executive Mansion, but it also came to be known as the President's House. As early as the 1820s its whitewashed exterior gave rise to its popular designation as the White House, and President Theodore Roosevelt made the name official shortly after he succeeded the assassinated William McKinley in 1901. The Executive Mansion was burned by the British during the War of 1812 and was rebuilt by Hoban. The West Wing was added by Teddy Roosevelt, the Oval Office by William Howard Taft, and the Truman Balcony was created when the entire building was gutted and rebuilt during Harry Truman's tenure to keep it from falling down. Numerous first ladies carried out extensive remodelings and devised new decorative approaches according to the styles of the time. The interior of the White House was at its most ornate during the latter part of the nineteenth century, according to the grand designs of Julia Grant. Teddy and Edith Roosevelt brought in Louis Comfort Tiffany to create an Art

Nouveau ambiance. More recently, Jackie Kennedy took a major step in restoring the house to a pre–Civil War elegance and reclaiming historic furnishings, a program continued by subsequent first ladies.

Many presidents have moved into the White House to find it threadbare and rundown. More than one first lady has felt it was in a condition more common to "second-class boardinghouses" than to the homes of even the average wealthy citizen. That in part is due to the hundreds of thousands of tourists who visit the President's House each year, as well as to the fact that it is also a nerve center of the United States government. But while Congress can usually be counted on to appropriate money to keep up appearances in the public rooms, the family quarters also suffer a great deal of wear and tear, especially when there are numerous presidential children or grandchildren on hand. The family quarters have been on the second floor from the start, but there were also offices located there during most of the nineteenth century. Calvin Coolidge had the roof raised in the 1920s to provide more family space in what had been storage rooms, and every inch of space has proved necessary over the years when large presidential families were in residence.

The dream of every major American politician has always been to live in the White House at 1600 Pennsylvania Avenue. But making it into a home has often proved as taxing a job as running the country. For it is not only the President's House but also the People's House. It belongs to the nation, not to the families that temporarily inhabit it — often for less time than they might wish. From the start, the White House has been both a "goldfish bowl" in one sense and a "jail" in another, and many members of presidential families have used both phrases to describe it. Because of the public's fascination with the White House occupants, the press has always tried to peer into the private lives of presidents and their wives and children, to the extent that the mansion's walls sometimes seem made of glass to the families living inside. But those families have always had to worry about their physical security, as well. There have always been deranged individuals with warped political agendas who have threatened presidents and their families with violence, and too often they have succeeded in inflicting it upon a president and a nation. In the White House itself, presidential families are safe, but that security comes at the cost of sometimes feeling imprisoned. It's difficult to turn a prison into a home.

The children of presidents have always helped to make the White House more of a home. In fact, it was a childless president, William McKinley, who first referred to the White House as "my jail." Older presidential children have inevitably been more aware of the pressures of the White House than the younger ones. The kids, who have ranged in age from newborns to boys and girls in their early teens, have always made the White House a more cheerful place. Their laughter and pranks have helped to buoy presidents even in the most difficult times. Abraham Lincoln's two younger sons were a great solace to him during the agony of the Civil War, and John F. Kennedy restored his spirits at the height of the Cuban Missile Crisis by lifting Caroline Kennedy into his lap and reading aloud to her.

Even the hard-working permanent heart of the White House, the White House staff — many of whom work within its walls for decades, watching numerous presidential families come and go — have made it clear in their memoirs that having young children in the White House gives its august rooms a fresh sense of life. Those children may sometimes make for extra work, with their childish demands and roughhousing, but they also give the President's House a human dimension that lifts everyone's spirits and makes it a happier place.

This book tells the stories of nearly two hundred years of White House kids. Much more is known about some children than others, especially in the earlier years, but even the lesser known ones have left their mark on the history of the President's House. They have left behind memories that are often funny and sometimes deeply moving. Their lives reflect the times they lived in and provide surprising insights into their parents, the presidents and first ladies who have led our nation. Whether it is the tale of a twelve-year-old's pony being taken upstairs to his sickroom in the White House elevator, of the pomp and circumstance surrounding the wedding of a president's daughter, or of coping with the assassination of one's father, the stories of the White House kids — the rascals and little darlings or the grown women who acted as their father's hostesses — are a part of the story of America. What the children and grandchildren did and felt in the President's House touches the lives of all of us.

2

∿

Rascals and Little Darlings

During the first six decades of the nineteenth century, the great majority of presidential offspring were adults by the time their fathers gained the White House. In fact, most of the young children or teenagers who lived in the White House were grandchildren. The press paid far less attention to children in the earlier part of the nineteenth century, and most of what is known about the White House kids of that era has been gleaned from the personal correspondence of female members of the presidents' families, whether first ladies or relatives who lived in or often visited the White House. There was less sentimentality about children then, in part because so many youngsters died before reaching adulthood. Scarlet fever, smallpox, and even milder childhood diseases like measles could easily prove fatal without the intervention of medical practices and drugs we now take for granted. Thus, however dearly parents might cherish their children, they tended to guard their emotions against the strong possibility that any child might die an early death. A more open sentimentality about children wouldn't develop until the latter half of the century, and the press was therefore far less interested in the activities of White House kids.

During the four months that John and Abigail Adams lived in the cold, drafty, and still unfinished White House (half the original thirty-six rooms were still unplastered) in the winter of 1801, the walls reverberated with the tantrums of their granddaughter, Susannah, who then and later was renowned for having an even worse temper than her grandfather the President. She was the child of the Adamses' third child, Charles, who had died of drink that winter at only twenty-nine. Their eldest son, John Quincy Adams, who would eventually become president himself, visited only once or twice, daughter Abigail not at all, and only Thomas, in his midtwenties, was a White House resident. Since Adams had been defeated by Thomas Jefferson in the November 1800 election, the family's stay in the President's House was a gloomy one, indeed.

Over the next half century, the White

House was often enlivened by the presence of grandchildren, two of whom were born in the White House — the first to Jefferson's daughter Maria and the second to John Quincy Adams's son John and his wife, Mary. But it was not until 1861 that the first well-known young children of a president took up residence in the White House. Abraham and Mary Todd Lincoln had three sons when he became president on the eve of the Civil War. The eldest was Robert Todd Lincoln, born on August 1, 1843, just nine months after his parents' marriage. A second son, Edward Baker Lincoln, was born March 10, 1845, but died on February 1, 1850, after an unknown illness that lasted fifty-two days. Mary Todd Lincoln had always had a nervous disposition, and the death of "little Eddie" was a terrible blow. But she went on to have two more sons, William Wallace Lincoln, born late the same year that Eddie died, on December 21, 1850, and Thomas Lincoln, always called Tad or Taddie, born April 4, 1853. Tad had a large head, which may have caused an injury to his mother during birth. She suffered from what she called "womanly problems" for another dozen years, although the problem was apparently somewhat mitigated by the onset of menopause.

The Lincolns doted on their children. Robert was extremely bright and matured early, though he lacked the humor and gaiety of which both parents were capable, despite Abe's tendency to melancholy and Mary's ever-growing susceptibility to a form of hysteria. During the first year of his father's presidency, Robert began attending Harvard, returning to the White House for vacations. But young Willie and Tad were among the liveliest of all the White House kids, alternately amusing and annoying the White House staff with their antics and providing the principal source of joy for their parents in the midst of the agonizing pressures of the Civil War.

Both parents agreed that Willie was much like his father, thoughtful and caring but with a mischievous sense of humor that would suddenly break through like a shaft of sunlight. Tad was more like his mother, high-strung and alternating between great good spirits and sudden depression. Soon after their arrival at the White House, Willie and Tad found fast friends in the two young sons of Judge and Mrs. Horatio N. Taft, Bud and Holly. The Tafts lived nearby, and the four boys were constantly racing back and forth between the two homes, with both families prepared to feed all four of them wherever they happened to be at mealtimes. The Tafts' daughter, Julia, in her late teens, was ostensibly in charge of keeping an eye on the boys during the first year that the Lincolns lived in the White House, but she would confess that the job was nearly impossible and utterly exhausting.

Mary Todd Lincoln biographer Ruth Painter Randall wrote of the cyclonic activities of the boys, "It was well that the White House was in stronger condition during the Lincoln administration than in the nineteen forties, for its historic timbers had a lot to take from the romping, clattering little figures that raced through it from roof to basement, and turned it into a warlike playhouse."

The flat roof of the White House, punctuated by chimneys, would often prove both a retreat and a playground for White House kids in the years to come, but Willie and Tad, together with the Taft boys, were the first to see its many possibilities. It could be a fort, with the chimneys used as defenses, or the deck of a ship, with sheets flapping in the breeze like sails. Here, atop the command post where their father was directing the fate of a nation and deciding on the movements of great armies and naval fleets, the boys played out a more innocent game of war.

On one occasion Willie and Tad decided to present a circus on the roof, charging five cents to anyone who wanted to view the spectacle — or could be dragooned into doing so. At the start of the performance, Tad made an impressive appearance as ringmaster, wearing his father's reading glasses. Lincoln's secretary, a military man who regarded the boys' behavior as generally outrageous, was forced to climb all the way up to the roof to retrieve the glasses so the President could get on with the nation's urgent business. The secretary was furious, but Lincoln himself later put in an appearance on the roof, dutifully paying the five-cent entrance fee. Such moments brought him much-cherished relief from grim reports of lost battles, enormous casualties, and desperate pleas for more men and supplies needed by the Union armies struggling to gain the upper hand from the Shenandoah Valley to the Mississippi River.

No one could predict what Tad would get up to next. He found the location of the mansion's bell system, and with Willie's help managed to set off the bells in every office at once, causing a mild panic as secretaries and aides rushed about trying to discover what they were so urgently needed to do. Tad thought nothing of bursting in on his father when he was working, with Willie and the Taft boys in tow on several occasions. Carl Sandburg describes how the four boys

took rags and old clothes and made a doll they named Jack. In red baggy trousers, with a tight blue jacket and a red fez on his head, this Jack was a Zouave [a unique regiment of Union soldiers]. And they sentenced Jack to be shot at sunrise for sleeping on picket duty. They were burying Jack when the head gardener asked, "Why don't you have Jack pardoned?" Into the White House chased the four boys, upstairs to a desk where a man dropped his work, heard them, and soberly wrote on a sheet of Executive Mansion stationery:

The doll Jack is pardoned
By order of the President
A. Lincoln

To Julia Taft, sister of Bud and Holly, Tad gave this pardon paper, saying there would be no burying of Jack. In a week, however, Jack was hanging from the branch of a big bush in the garden, Tad saying, "Jack was a traitor and a spy."

Willie, three years older, was more studious, polite, and gentler than Tad, and he often made attempts to reign in Tad's wildness — which today would clearly be seen as a case of hyperactivity. But according to many accounts, Willie also couldn't stand to see his sometimes moody younger brother unhappy. So he would join Tad in his prankster schemes and try to think up ways to cheer up his brother when a bad mood set in. Lizzie Todd Grimsley, Mary Todd Lincoln's cousin, spent the first six months of the Lincoln presidency living at the White House and helping Mrs. Lincoln get acclimated to her new surroundings, even though Mrs. Grimsley had her own family back home in Ohio. She later wrote a book about her experiences, and told of Tad dissolving into tears because of an incident that occurred when he accompanied his mother on one of her almost daily visits to Union soldiers camped around Washington or hospitalized in the city.

On this day, instead of bringing flowers as usual, Tad proudly passed out Union propaganda pamphlets. The soldiers laughed at him — not unkindly, but because they were amused by this small boy's attempt to further his father's political message. Tad went home to the White House and tearfully related the story. Willie, standing by, was obviously thinking deeply, and he suddenly looked up at his father, his face brightening. "There!" said Lincoln, "you have it now, have you not?" According to Mrs. Grimsley, he recognized that Willie had figured out a way to console his brother. Lincoln then turned to a visitor and said, "I know every process by which that boy arrived at his satisfactory solution of the question before him, as it is by just such slow methods that I attain results."

Willie was also possessed of his father's natural courtesy. When Prince Napoleon, the nephew of Napoleon III, emperor of France from 1852–70, came to Washington, the Lincolns gave a dinner party for him, but through some mix-up, no one was at the door to greet him. "Instead," Jean H. Baker writes in *Mary Todd Lincoln*, "it was the imperturbable Willie Lincoln who did the honors, bowing low to French royalty with the majesty of which the third Lincoln son was capable." Even earlier, back home in Springfield, Illinois, friends of the Lincolns had noted the special qualities of Willie Lincoln. In Washington, Julia Taft — despite being run ragged by Tad, Willie, and her brothers — called Willie "the most lovable boy I ever knew."

It was thus with great alarm that the

household reacted to Willie's sudden illness on February 7, 1863, after he'd been riding his pony. It is now thought that he contracted typhoid fever, always a danger in the swampy Washington locale. And then Tad, too, became sick. Willie seemed to be getting better but then had a relapse, while Tad held his own. It is likely that Willie's system had been weakened by an earlier case of scarlet fever, which often damaged the heart. Bud Taft would come sit by his friend's bedside, holding his hand, sometimes falling asleep there. A highly distraught Mary Lincoln went back and forth between her two sick sons. Even those who had complained about the undisciplined racket caused by the Lincoln boys were chastened by the dreadful silence that had descended on the White House.

Daily dispatches on his brothers' conditions were sent to Robert Lincoln at Harvard, and newspapers across the country began to spread the news of the two boys' illnesses. By February 17, after Willie had been ill for ten days, the press began to use the word "hopeless" to describe his state. He died on February 20, 1862. Carl Sandburg quotes from a letter written by Elizabeth Keckley, "the mulatto seamstress and Mrs. Lincoln's trusted companion," who assisted in washing and dressing the dead Willie. She had just finished when President Lincoln came into the room: "He lifted the cover from the face of his child, gazed at it long, and murmured, 'It is hard, hard, hard to have him die!' "

Willie's White House funeral was attended by senators, cabinet officers, foreign ministers, and soldiers, but Mary Lincoln was too overcome to appear. Never again would she set foot in the room where he had died or in the Green Room, where he had been embalmed. It would be months before she once more took up her daily rounds visiting soldiers and still longer before the White House entertained guests.

With Willie gone, Tad became even more rambunctious at times. Carl Sandburg writes, "A party of Boston ladies one day admired the velvet carpet, plush upholstery, mahogany furniture and pompous chandeliers of the East Room. The air was quiet, dignified. Then a slam-bang racket, a shrill voice, 'Look out there!' — and young Tad came through flourishing a long whip, driving two goats hitched tandem to a kitchen chair."

Tad loved animals and one goat in particular, whom he called Nanny. But Nanny met a mysterious end. Tad had made an enemy of the head gardener, Major Watt, by eating every single strawberry being forced in the greenhouse for a state dinner. Nanny had also taken to eating the flowers in the formal beds around the White House. Lincoln himself wrote to his wife, when she was away on a trip with Tad, about Nanny's disappearance. "The day you left, Nanny was found resting herself, and chewing her little cud, in the middle of Tad's bed. But now she's gone! The gardener kept complaining that she destroyed the flowers, 'til it was concluded to bring her down to the White House. This was done, and the second day she disappeared, and has not been heard of since." In her biography of Mary Lincoln, Ruth Painter Randall quotes this letter from the Lincoln Papers, dated August 8, 1863, adding, "One has one's suspicions about that gardener."

Tad also had a pony that he rode when his father reviewed troops, wearing the miniature uniform of a colonel, which he had begged for until his father acquiesced. Fortunately, the Union soldiers found the presence of this very "junior" officer amusing, although there are indications that some actual colonels were much less entertained. In 1864 Tad saved a turkey from the dinner menu and adopted it as a pet. On election day, November 8, 1864, Tad and his father watched the soldiers in the camps surrounding the White House from the second floor of the mansion, as they chose between reelecting President Lincoln and putting in his place General George B. McLellan, who had been very popular as the commander of the Union Army but whom Lincoln had fired because he so often demanded more troops instead of launching attacks against the Confederate forces. As the President and Tad watched the voting, they noticed the pet turkey, called Jack (like the Zouave doll Tad had once "executed"), wandering among the soldiers. Lincoln asked Tad whether Jack could vote, making a small joke on a very tense day, and Tad replied, "He is underage." Happily, Lincoln didn't need Jack's vote; the soldiers strongly supported him over their former commander.

For all his antics, Tad was also known for his caring nature. He collected books to send to soldiers in the Washington camps at Christmas in 1863, explaining to his father that they looked terribly lonely and that it might help to have something to read. The following Christmas he went out of the White House and rounded up a group of street urchins and brought them in to Christmas dinner. He also personally saw to it that at least one family was reunited. As Carl Sandburg tells it, "The guard Crook took note of a woman intercepting Tad in a corridor, telling Tad her boys and girls were cold and starving because their father was shut up in prison and couldn't work for them. Tad ran to his father with the story. The father sat at a desk with papers, an absent look on his face, and said he would look into the case as soon as he had time. Tad clung to his father's knees and begged till his father listened. And Tad ran back and told the woman her husband would be set free. The woman blessed him and cried, and Tad cried, and Crook said he had to cry, too."

On April 9, 1865, General Robert E. Lee surrendered the Army of Northern Virginia to General Ulysses S. Grant at Appomattox, and the Civil War was at last over. On the evening of April 11 a vast crowd assembled outside the White House to hear Lincoln read a speech. The President extolled General Grant and his men, then turned soberly to the subject of reconstruction, using that word. The crowd was somewhat surprised by this note of reconciliation. Lincoln was having some difficulty reading the speech by candlelight, and as he finished with each page, he let it flutter to the ground, where

Tad bent to pick each sheet up, calling softly each time for "another" and "another."

Three days later, on Good Friday, April 14, President and Mrs. Lincoln attended the theater. They had done that a hundred times or more over the previous five years. Often they went to Grover's Theater, which put on opera and minstrel shows as well as dramas. On some occasions they took Tad along with them. "Once in '64," Carl Sandburg writes, "Tad quietly slipped away from a box at Grover's. And soon the father saw his boy on stage with a chorus singing 'The Battle Cry of Freedom,' Tad half lost in a Union Army blue uniform blouse."

But on this Good Friday, Tad stayed at the White House as his father somewhat reluctantly accompanied his wife to Ford's Theater to see Laura Keene in *Our American Cousin*. There, President Lincoln was shot by John Wilkes Booth. Grievously wounded in the head, he was carried to a house across the street. A hysterical Mary Lincoln insisted that Tad be brought from the White House to his father's bedside, since Lincoln always responded to Tad's voice. But even Tad could not get through to him, and the President died nine hours later.

There had always been those who thought that the Lincolns spoiled Tad terribly, giving in to his whims too easily and disciplining him far too infrequently. But others recognized how much both Tad and Willie Lincoln meant to their parents, how important the boys were in maintaining their parents' equilibrium in a terrible time. Among those in the press who understood, perhaps none expressed it better than a reporter from the *St. Cloud Democrat,* who visited Washington to attend a Union meeting at which the President and various cabinet members gave speeches. Tad was there — Lincoln often took him along where small boys would not usually be allowed — and growing tired and bored, he climbed up on his father's lap. The reporter wrote: "As the long, bony hand spread out over the dark hair, and the thin face above rested the sharp chin upon it, it was a pleasant sight. The head of a great and powerful nation . . . soothing with loving care the little restless creature so much dearer than all the power he wields. . . ."

The next two presidents, Andrew Johnson and Ulysses S. Grant, both had young sons as well as older children, but neither Andrew Johnson Jr., who was ten when his father succeeded the assassinated Lincoln, nor Jesse Grant, who was eleven when his father became president in 1868, attracted much public attention. In Andrew's case he was just one child among many, since he was surrounded by nephews and nieces his own age or younger. They were the children of his oldest sister, Mary Stover, whose husband had been killed in the war, and of his sister Martha Patterson, wife of the new senator from Tennessee. In this hubbub, Andrew kept a low profile. He was a serious child, undoubtedly affected by his harrowing experiences during the war. While his father was on the move as the military governor, Andrew and his mother had been forced to flee their simple family home when the area came under attack by Confederate forces. Eliza McCardle Johnson and her then seven-year-old son, Andrew Jr., spent seven months as homeless wanderers in the Tennessee mountains, begging for food from the poor homesteaders in the hills.

Jesse Grant would say in a book he wrote nearly fifty years later that the White House was "the best playground in the world," but he provided few details about his life there. It is known that he had a telescope on the roof and that his father sometimes joined him there to gaze at the stars. And, like so many White House kids before and after, he had a pony to ride, but his activities were overshadowed by his older sister, Ellen — known as Nellie — whose White House wedding is described in Chapter Four.

The young White House child who attracted the most attention in the years following the Civil War was Fanny Hayes. When Rutherford B. Hayes became president in 1877, Fanny was ten. Her younger brother, Scott, just eight, and her older brother Webb, twenty-one, also lived in the White House. Two other brothers visited only occasionally. Birch, twenty-four, was already a practicing attorney in Ohio, and Rud, nineteen, was at college. Webb served as his father's confidential secretary and carried a gun for his father's protection. But it was Fanny who got her name into the newspapers most often.

Fanny loved dollhouses, and the large upper hallway was so cluttered with them that it made life difficult for the cleaning staff. But Fanny seemed to be able to use her charm to get what she wanted. She had a special knack for getting distinguished artists to give her presents. The German-American painter Albert Bierstadt, whose enormous mural *The Settlement of California* decorates the Capitol to this day, created a special gift for Fanny while on a White House visit, right in front of her eyes. The artist cut a large sheet of paper into the shape of a butterfly, applied various colors of paint to one half of it, and then folded the other half over. When opened, the paint had created beautiful patterns. A delighted Fanny had the huge butterfly hung in the north corridor, which served as a schoolroom where she and Scott were privately tutored.

William Rutherford Mead, a cousin of the President and a partner in the New York architectural firm that would later be responsible for expanding the White House during Theodore Roosevelt's occupancy, was prevailed upon for a more lavish gift. He designed and had built for Fanny a Queen Anne bedroom set in black lacquer, which was very much the "latest thing" in styles. Fanny's Washington friends were agog — and no doubt tried to pressure their own parents into providing a similar luxury. But although Rutherford B. Hayes was by far the wealthiest president of the nineteenth century, his children were not really spoiled. Even Fanny, who seemed to be able to charm everyone, was described by her father in his diary as "very sensible, does not take jokes, defends her absent friends, is like

Mother Hayes."

Hayes's account of his daughter's twelfth birthday party on September 2, 1879, makes clear his affection for her: "Our darling's birthday. We have tried to make it a happy one, and certainly it is her best. . . . She had a bevy of her young friends to lunch and dine with her. . . . Her presents are, Lady of the Lake, Encyclopedia of Poetry, Whittier's Poems, a casket [decorative china box], Paper Knife, Jewelry."

Fanny and her younger brother, Scott, were very close, their father noted, and often did things together. In 1880 Hayes wrote in his diary that two nights earlier Fanny and Scott "appeared at a costume ball for children given by their dancing master. Fanny was beautiful as Martha Washington, and Scott as an orderly Sergeant of the 23rd [Regiment, Ohio Volunteer Infantry]. Fanny copied the picture in the East Room." On another occasion Hayes wrote about having William M. Evarts, the secretary of state, to lunch when all of his family except the two youngest were away. "Fanny presided at the tea pot. Scott filled up the table!"

While Fanny received more attention from the press by far, the President paid just as close attention to his even younger son.

In December of 1876, when the results of the presidential election that had pitted him against Samuel J. Tilden were still in doubt because of voting irregularities — which it took a special electoral commission to resolve in Hayes's favor by one vote — Hayes wrote in his diary:

Today Scott was heard reading, as he pretended, to his sister very solemnly as follows . . . "R.B. Hayes is elected and the Democrats will kill him. A monument will be built and on it will be

R.B. Hayes
Killed by the Democrats

And they will kill all of the Republicans. If Tilden is elected the State will go to ruin."
This shows how a six year old looks at the crisis.

While Hayes was clearly amused at his son's imaginings, this passage helps to explain why his twenty-one-year-old son, Webb, carried a gun in the White House. It also makes clear that even very young children are more aware than many people may think of the political problems faced by fathers who are involved in presidential politics. They can't escape such knowledge. Yet at other times they are just children, and they must be schooled in more normal concerns. In June of 1878 Hayes confided to his diary, "I have walked with Scott many mornings lately. He seems to be fond of learning. I have taught him in our walks, items of the Calendar — days of the year, month &c &c and today the year — 1878 — and the reason for it. He is not a 'smart' boy — but sound and promising."

Only three presidents, John Quincy Adams, James K. Polk, and Rutherford B. Hayes, kept personal, as opposed to official, diaries while they lived in the White House, and Hayes's is by far the most detailed about the social and daily life of a first family. But for all the affection he expresses for his children, perhaps the single clearest picture of the relationship he enjoyed with Fanny and Scott, as well as with his grown sons, was provided in a letter home from Dora Scott, a cousin of Mrs. Hayes who paid a lengthy visit to the White House. She was both charmed and amused by the repeated scenes of the President of the United States peeling an apple at the dining table, cutting it into sections, and then tossing the sections with great accuracy around the table for his children to catch.

The first White House kids to be subjected to the prying lens of newspaper photographers were the grandchildren of Benjamin Harrison, who served from 1887–1893. There had been earlier photographs of White House kids, including a famous one of Tad Lincoln in his miniature colonel's uniform, but they were posed pictures for which elaborate arrangements had to be made. By the late 1880s, however, cameras had developed to the point where "candid" shots could be snapped at any time. There were three Harrison grandchildren who were often at the White House, but the press favorite was little Benjamin McKee, the son of the President's daughter Mary. Like the Kennedy children seventy years later, "Baby McKee," as the newspapers dubbed him, was likely to crawl or toddle into view in the midst of serious presidential business. He was not quite two when his grandfather became president. As he grew, pictures were also snapped of him chasing — or being chased by — his pet goat on the White House lawn.

In part because of this attention by the press, Grover Cleveland and his wife, Frances, went to extreme lengths to avoid letting reporters near their children when they moved into the White House in 1893. Grover Cleveland had served a previous term as president, was defeated by Harrison, and then won the rematch in 1892, becoming the only president to serve two nonconsecutive terms. Cleveland had been a bachelor when elected to his first term, then married the lovely young Frances Folsom in 1886. He was then forty-nine, and she was twenty-two. Their first child, Ruth, was born in 1891, just before they moved back into the White House. Another daughter, Esther, arrived in 1893, the only presidential child to be born in the White House itself, although a number of presidential grandchildren had been born there.

Early in Cleveland's second term, Frances Cleveland had watched from the White House windows as a group of tourists tried to grab little Ruth from her nurse's arms on the South Lawn, apparently to get a better look at her. The Clevelands had disapproved of the pictures of Baby McKee that had appeared in newspapers across the land, and this incident on the lawn further increased their determination to keep their daughters out of sight. So completely absent from public view were they, rumors spread that Esther had been born deformed. According to the author of

The President's House, William Seale, "the Clevelands were so adamant about the privacy of their children that they did not even attempt to correct the stories."

Thus almost nothing is known of their White House experiences. Seale reports that as a grown woman, Esther went there as a guest:

Nothing she saw made her recall anything about her first four years of life. But when she entered the family quarters on the second floor, she was struck by a strong recollection of the fragrance of roses, together with mustiness. Back home she asked her mother if she remembered anything curious about the upstairs of the White House. Mrs. Cleveland thought back over the years and replied yes. "That one floor had the smell of an old house by the sea, a musty scent, overlaid with roses."

There is widespread agreement that the most interesting child of a president ever to live in the White House was Alice Roosevelt, the eldest child of Theodore Roosevelt and the only offspring of his first marriage to Alice Lee Roosevelt. Her mother died of Bright's Disease (which would now be entirely treatable) in the same year that Alice was born, 1884. Her father remarried in

1886, and his second wife, Edith, bore him five more children. Theodore, called Ted, was only three years younger than Alice, born in 1887. Then came Kermit (1889), Ethel (1891), Archibald, called "Archie" (1894), and Quentin (1897).

In *Mrs. L: Conversations with Alice Roosevelt Longworth*, published in 1981, Michael Teague sets down Alice's memories of her childhood. "We were quite close as a family but inevitably there was a pairing off," Alice recalled. "Ted and I were boon companions and shared many of the same interests. Kermit couldn't have been more fun, especially as he grew older. He paired off with Ethel. Quentin and Archie were 'the little boys.' Quentin in particular had tremendous charm and I was devoted to him." Alice gave her father credit for paying a great deal of attention to his children. "I don't suppose any parent ever participated more actively in the pastimes of his children than my father did." She remembered that when he was away he wrote "wonderful picture letters. . . . After he became President we used to say, 'Do us one of those so we can cash them in later.' We called them 'Posterity Letters.' "

Theodore Roosevelt was the youngest man ever to become president, at the age of forty-two, after serving only six months as William McKinley's vice president. Mc-Kinley died on September 14, 1901, a week after being shot by anarchist Leon Czolgoz in Buffalo, New York. McKinley was beloved by the American people, but the Roosevelt children had a different view of him and actively disliked his invalid wife. Ever frank, Alice admitted to Michael Teague, "When we learned of McKinley's attempted assassination, we put on long faces and then my brother [Ted] and I went outside and did a little jig." If this sounds irreverent, it is in keeping with Alice Roosevelt's utterly candid assessment of even living presidents during her long lifetime. She had first visited the White House when she was only six, to be introduced to Benjamin Harrison, "who appeared to me a gnarled, bearded gnome of a man gloomily ensconced in a corner of the Red Room. . . ." This description is perfectly harmonious with Harrison's own views — he openly referred to the White House as "my jail."

When the Roosevelt clan took up residence, the White House was subjected to a clatter it hadn't experienced since Tad and Willie Lincoln and their friends Bud and Holly Taft had raced wildly through it forty years earlier. The Oval Office would not be built for another ten years, and both the presidential offices and the family rooms were on the second floor. "There was a staircase at the end," Alice recounted to Michael Teague, "which led down to the main hall. We used to slide down it on large tin trays from the pantry. Stilts and bicycles were allowed in the upstairs hall but not downstairs. We were forbidden the downstairs rooms when they were open to the public. Otherwise, we pretty well had the run of the place. We loved it when the large potted palms sprouting out of the overstuffed circular seats in the East Room were removed and we could use the vacant space to launch surprise assaults on each other and anyone else who happened to be passing by."

Alice was seventeen when she moved into the White House, on the verge of becoming a great beauty but still full of girlish mischief. The public was fascinated by her, and the newspapers were constantly full of tales about her. The press never did find out about her habit of sneaking up to the White House roof to smoke cigarettes — a truly scandalous activity for a young lady at that period. But a great deal was made of Alice's pet garter snake, Emily Spinach, so called because it was as green as spinach and as thin as her maiden Aunt Emily. Alice carried the snake with her in a stocking box — appropriate housing for a garter snake — but the stories became exaggerated "until one would have thought I was harboring a boa constrictor in the White House." Her friends wouldn't let her into their homes with it, and one day she found it dead in its box. It had obviously not died of natural causes. "I was so furious, I couldn't see straight for weeks."

It was in connection with Emily Spinach that President Roosevelt made the most famous remark ever uttered by a president about a White House kid. One day he was visited at the White House by his good friend Owen Wister, author of the best-selling novel *The Virginian*, which was later made into the classic Gary Cooper movie of 1929 and served as the basis of the 1950s television series. Stories about Alice and Emily Spinach were all over the newspapers, and Wister teased the President by asking why he couldn't control his daughter better. Roosevelt replied, "I can do one of two things. I can be President of the United States or I can control Alice. I cannot possibly do both."

Soon, however, Alice would mature into a

poised and beautiful young woman whom her father would send to China and Japan as his personal representative. But she did not give up smoking on the White House roof, and her younger brothers and sister also kept the White House a lively place, particularly Archie and Quentin. The President wrote to a friend that "Archie is a little trump, so loving and polite and honorable." That may have been how Roosevelt saw him, since the boy was always on his best behavior in front of his father, but he had a reputation for being "pugnacious" when his father wasn't looking. Archie and his good friend Charlie Taft, whose father William Howard Taft was secretary of war and would succeed Teddy Roosevelt as president in 1909, dashed around the White House with a speed that would have done Tad Lincoln proud.

In April of 1903 Archie came down with mumps and whooping cough simultaneously. The nine-year-old was not a model patient, but he was too sick to do much more than moan. He was also depressed about the death of Jack Dog, a black-and-tan fox terrier that had been his favorite. Little Quentin, whom his father called "a handful," devised a way to cheer up his brother. Quentin persuaded a White House footman to help him coax Archie's calico pony, named Algonquin, into the White House elevator. In her biography of First Lady Edith Roosevelt, Sylvia Jukes Morris describes this endeavor:

The 350-pound animal was understandably nervous at first, but soon became interested in his own reflection in the elevator mirror, enabling the footman to press the second-floor button. The sight of Algonquin trotting into Archie's bedroom did wonders for the invalid, who immediately began to mend. In no time at all, he was up and dressed in his riding costume of Rough Rider hat, blue knickerbockers, and yellow leggings, and galloping around the White House grounds again.

Morris also reports on the virtual menagerie of other White House pets during the Roosevelt years. Although Alice's Emily Spinach was the most written about in the press, she also had a blue macaw named Eli, who spent most of his time in the conservatory but sometimes escaped to join Loretta the parrot in turning the corridors into a hazardous flight corridor. Visitors to the White House also had to look to their ankles, which might suddenly be seized either by Tom Quartz the cat or Josiah the badger.

And Kermit's kangaroo rat was likely to show up at the dining table, demanding lumps of sugar. The White House usher, Ike Hoover, later recalled, "A nervous person had no business around the White House in those days. He was sure to be a wreck in a very short time."

Kermit, however, was the quietest of the Roosevelt brood. "Very few outsiders care for him," according to his mother, to whom he was very close, "but if they like him at all, they like him very much." Kermit was a great reader and had bought a copy of the first book of poetry by the young Maine writer Edwin Arlington Robinson. He liked it so much, he insisted that his parents must read it. They, too, were impressed, the President to the extent that he found a post for the poet in the New York Treasury. It paid two thousand dollars a year and required little work. Kermit, and the President, had picked a real winner: Robinson would be awarded three Pulitzer Prizes over the years.

Although Kermit was the quiet one in the Roosevelt family, he was in much the same mold as such subsequent White House kids as Charlie Taft and the two Coolidge boys, John and Calvin Jr. Free from the disruptive influence of Archie Roosevelt, Charlie Taft was found to be a charmingly well-behaved

White House kid. According to White House military aide Captain Archibald Willingham Butt, who wrote hundreds of letters to his mother about both the Roosevelts and the Tafts, Charlie, his college-age sister, Helen, and eldest brother, Robert, showed no "sign of what might be called a 'swelled head.' They have inherited the kindly genial nature of the President and the hard common sense of the mother."

The Roosevelt children were thus the last group of White House kids whose antics regularly made the newspapers until half a century later, when the country became besotted with the even younger Kennedy children. Other presidential offspring would make an impact in different ways, but Teddy Roosevelt's kids were undoubtedly the liveliest group in the first half of the twentieth century.

3

∾

Festivities

Many of the most joyful occasions in the history of the White House have revolved around Christmas parties for young children. The first several presidents had Christmas parties that were attended by grandchildren, but the first large-scale celebration devoted particularly to children was held by Andrew Jackson on December 19, 1835. Jackson's wife, Rachel, had died three months before his first inauguration in 1829, and their adopted son, who had been given the name Andrew Jackson Jr., was a young man by then. But Jackson had countless grandnieces and grandnephews, and he encouraged them to visit the White House whenever possible.

The party he gave in 1835, toward the end of his second term, was for a large group of these youngsters as well as for the small children of cabinet officers, members of

Congress, and other prominent Washingtonians. The extent to which Jackson was able to command others to dance to his preferred tune of the moment was illustrated by the antics of Martin Van Buren, then the vice president and soon to be elected president in his own right. Not only did he stand on one leg and sing a children's song for the assembled youngsters, but he also proceeded to run around the room gobbling like a turkey for the amusement of the young guests. He, too, was a widower, and his own four sons were grown, but it seemed there was nothing he wouldn't do to gain Andrew Jackson's endorsement in the 1836 election. Jackson did indeed back him for good political reasons, but there is little doubt that Van Buren's willingness to make a fool of himself for the assembled children that Christmas played its part in gaining Old Hickory's blessing.

In 1878 Lucy Webb Hayes invited two daughters of John Herron, a long-time Ohio friend, to come to Washington for Christmas. The girls were in their early teens, a little older than Fanny Hayes, then eleven. The White House Christmas festivities delighted the Herron girls, and before she left, Helen Herron told Mrs. Hayes that she wanted to come back to the White

House someday as first lady herself. Helen married William Howard Taft when she grew up and was instrumental in persuading her husband, who really wanted to be chief justice (and one day would be), to run for the presidency as Teddy Roosevelt's anointed successor in 1908. Her childhood wish came true, and she presided over Christmas in the White House from 1911–1914. Helen Taft's eldest son, Robert — who would later become known as "Mr. Republican" — tried three times to gain the Republican nomination for president, with the aim of having his own White House Christmases, but he did not succeed.

Christmas as we know it did not become fully established until the late nineteenth century, and the first White House Christmas tree was put up in 1889. Benjamin and Caroline Harrison's four grandchildren were visiting the White House for Christmas, and the President was determined to make the holiday a happy time in the house that he referred to as "my jail." Late on Christmas Eve, the doors to the Oval Library were locked, and the President worked with the head gardener and other members of the White House staff to decorate a tree to surprise his grandchildren with the next morning.

There almost wasn't a Christmas tree the first year that Teddy Roosevelt occupied the White House, in 1901. Roosevelt was the first conservationist president in the modern sense, and he created many national parks and wildlife preserves. He was therefore disapproving of the idea of having a cut tree brought indoors at Christmastime. But Alice, Ted, Kermit, Ethel, Archie, and Quentin Roosevelt were equally determined to have one, regardless of their father's ideas, and they secretly put up a small tree in the family quarters. Roosevelt didn't have the heart to object too strenuously when he discovered it fully decorated. And he was subsequently informed by the head of the U.S. Forestry Service (which he created) that cutting some trees was actually good for those that were left. After that, a full-size Christmas tree once again reigned at the White House.

The Roosevelts had Christmas trees in abundance in 1903, when they gave a party for 550 Washington children under the age of twelve. Only Archie and Quentin Roosevelt were still under the age limit, but Ethel and Alice took part in keeping order among the excited young guests. The Marine Band played carols as the children entered with their mothers and nannies. The mothers were entertained in three separate parlors while the nannies were offered refreshments in the large basement hall. The children themselves were escorted to the East Room and regaled by a well-known singing and dancing group from Chicago known as Toney's Boys.

In *The President's House*, William Seale describes the tumult that followed.

At the instant Toney's Boys made their exit, President and Mrs. Roosevelt appeared at the hall door to the East Room and invited the crowd to march with them to the dining room for punch and cookies. The band played, and the scramble began. Chairs were overturned as the mob surged toward the hall, following the President's prancing steps in glee to the State Dining Room, where they found the table piled high with sweets. When the children had eaten their fill, the Roosevelts began to wonder what to do with them, for the party had yet an hour to go. Urged back to the East Room, now emptied of the chairs and platform, the little company ran wild across the great polished floor until the nurses and nannies had to be called up from the basement corridor to put a stop to the carnival and calm down their charges.

Given the daily antics of the Roosevelt children, it was only appropriate that this Christmas party should turn into a near riot.

Another famous White House Christmas party took place in 1923. Grace and Calvin Coolidge's teenage sons, John and Calvin Jr., were both attending Mercersberg Academy in New Jersey. When the family had moved to Washington in 1921, when Calvin Coolidge was sworn in as President Warren G. Harding's vice president, Grace Coolidge had insisted that her sons attend dancing school. They were not enthusiastic at first, but John in particular became a very good dancer, and he and his mother would often whirl into a waltz or foxtrot whenever there was music playing. The 1923 Christmas party was given for John and Cal Jr. and sixty boys from Mercersberg Academy. As a small orchestra played, Grace Coolidge danced with each and every boy attending the party.

Herbert and Lou Hoover and Franklin and Eleanor Roosevelt always had grandchildren at the White House at Christmastime. The Hoovers gave an annual Christmas Eve party, making sure that the guest list included enough children so that each adult present could be led in to dinner in the State

Dining Room by a child. On Christmas Eve 1929, the party was given as usual despite the Great Crash of October 1929. But as the Hoovers and their guests were eating dinner, a fire broke out in the Executive Office Building, now referred to as the West Wing. It had been remodeled by President Taft in 1909 and included the addition of the Oval Office. It also contained the Cabinet Room and dozens of smaller offices where the real work of the White House was done.

As the men rushed from the State Dining Room to see what help they could offer, Mrs. Hoover gathered her grandchildren and the many small guests their age around her by the Christmas tree at one end of the room, telling stories and passing out presents as the fire raged. The Hoovers' younger son, Allan, home from Harvard for the holidays, rushed to the Oval Office with one of his father's secretaries, pulling the drawers out of his father's desk, yanking pictures down from the walls, and getting as much out into the snow as possible before the Oval Office went up in flames. In later years, Allan would say that the White House had always given him "the willies." Given the horrors of that Christmas Eve, it's hardly a surprising statement. The Oval Office was rebuilt, and the entire complex was redesigned.

The most remarkable of the Christmases that Franklin and Eleanor Roosevelt spent in the White House in the company of their grown children and many grandchildren came in 1941. The attack on Pearl Harbor on December 7 by the Japanese had finally brought the United States into World War II, and Washington was under very heavy security. Back in 1923 Calvin Coolidge had begun the tradition of having a "Community Christmas Tree" in Lafayette Park across from the White House, which the resident president or first lady, accompanied by their children or grandchildren, had lit every Christmas since then. But the military didn't want to attract the attention of possible German saboteurs or even bombers and tried to persuade FDR to forgo the tree. Roosevelt refused, agreeing only to have it moved inside the White House fence, and that year it was called the National Christmas Tree for the first time.

That Christmas was also notable for the presence of a White House guest who had arrived secretly from England. The guest was Winston Churchill, and his presence was made known on Christmas Eve, when he and President Roosevelt made a joint radio broadcast to the nation from the White House. Mindful of the moment, of the Roosevelt grandchildren gathered at the White House, and of the millions of children who would be listening across the continent, Churchill said in his famous voice, "Let the children have their night of fun and laughter. Let the gifts of Father Christmas delight their hearts. Let us share in their unstinted pleasure before we turn to the stern tasks in the year that lies before us."

For more than a hundred years, the annual White House Easter Egg Roll has also been a festive occasion for the younger children, or the grandchildren, of presidents — even if their mothers have often viewed it as one of the more taxing duties of their job as first lady. The Easter event was originally held on Capitol Hill, probably beginning well before the Civil War. Washington children would show up on the appointed day with baskets of colored eggs to roll down the steep incline. As children raced about shrieking with joy and getting into the occasional fistfight, they brought a degree of liveliness to the august precincts of the Capitol grounds that was echoed within the halls of Congress only during the most passionate political debates. Congress increasingly found the event too raucous for its taste and in 1876 passed a law prohibiting any kind of playground activity in the vicinity of the Capitol.

It was suggested that the festivities be moved to the White House lawn, and President Hayes gave his permission. It is believed that his young daughter Fanny was instrumental in persuading him to turn the White House lawn into a public playground for an afternoon, and it has been a traditional celebration ever since. The younger White House kids always looked forward to this Easter Monday occasion. In 1903 Archie Roosevelt's simultaneous bout with mumps and whooping cough coincided with the Easter Egg Roll, deepening his sickbed gloom considerably.

Older presidential children delighted in watching the spectacle, and first family pets often got into the act, as well. President Coolidge — despite the possible damage to his dour demeanor — would dress up his dogs in bonnets and ribbons and take them for a stroll in the midst of the melee. And "melee" was exactly the word that many first ladies have used to describe the event. However much her children enjoyed it, Edith Roosevelt commented that it seemed "[s]uch needless destruction of the lovely grass." She was not amused by the game many children played called "picking eggs"

— smacking eggs together to see whose cracked first. The resulting smell, Edith noted, permeated the air for several blocks.

These days, for security reasons, only invited children may attend the Easter Egg Roll, although an effort is made to see that poor children are included as well as the sons and daughters of the Washington elite. Children love the event, and the press revels in it, but the White House dreads it. But frankness on the subject doesn't surface until an administration is on the way out. When Bill Clinton was elected in the fall of 1992, there was much talk in the press about how much policy-making Hillary Rodham Clinton would be involved in. An aide to outgoing First Lady Barbara Bush was quoted as saying that first ladies had more than enough to do without getting involved in policy and suggested that Mrs. Clinton would be stunned to discover what a "living hell" the annual Easter Egg Roll could be. Nevertheless, White House kids from Fanny Hayes to Amy Carter have found it enormous fun.

A number of the adult daughters of presidents have found themselves in charge of Christmas parties and the Easter Egg Roll as well as the arrangements for official dinners for the Washington elite or foreign heads of state. Several nineteenth-century presidents, including Thomas Jefferson, Andrew Jackson, and Martin Van Buren, were widowers; in other cases the first lady was not physically well enough to carry out the extensive entertaining required by their position. Sometimes a daughter-in-law acted as the president's hostess. These grown women were hardly "kids," but some of their stories are of special interest and demonstrate the degree to which the children of presidents are inevitably drawn into the center of their father's political lives.

One of the most interesting of these substitute first ladies was Priscilla Cooper Tyler, the wife of President John Tyler's eldest son, Robert. President Tyler's wife, Letitia, had borne her husband seven children. She suffered a stroke in 1839 but moved to Washington with him and their children when he became vice president in 1841, serving with President William Henry Harrison. Harrison delivered the longest inaugural address, lasting more than two hours, in very cold weather, caught pneumonia, and died within a month of becoming president, and Vice President Tyler was thrust into the presidency. Letitia Tyler was far too weak to serve as a hostess when her husband succeeded Harrison, and he called on his son Robert's young wife, Priscilla, to take charge. She was more than up to the job.

Priscilla was the daughter of Thomas A. Cooper, one of America's most famous actors, who specialized in playing Shakespeare's tragic heroes. His daughter had often performed with him and was extremely pretty, poised, and well educated. She took on all the duties of first lady, devising menus and seating charts and sending out invitations, then presiding at social functions. Far from finding this a heavy duty, she would later write that it had been "the pleasantest part of my life." John Tyler was a wealthy man, and he saw to it that his daughter-in-law looked the part she was playing, hiring dressmakers to provide her with silk ball gowns with long trains. "On the President's arm," writes William Seale, "she entered the East Room during receptions, proudly fulfilling her grandest role." She served in this capacity for two years. Tyler's wife, Letitia, attended only one social occasion, the wedding of her eighteen-year-old daughter Elizabeth in early 1842. Mrs. Tyler died of another stroke in September of that year. Just before the end of his term, John Tyler married again, choosing as his bride Julia Gardner, who was thirty years younger and who subsequently bore him another seven children. Julia of course took over the duties of first lady as soon as she was married, and Priscilla's "grandest role" was behind her.

Another success as substitute first lady was scored by a very different young woman, Andrew Johnson's daughter Martha. Her mother, Eliza McArdle Johnson, was very frail, in part due to her harrowing experiences wandering the hills of Tennessee for seven months during the Civil War. Martha had been born in a log cabin but had gone to Washington with her parents when Andrew Johnson served in Congress starting in the late 1840s. She attended the Academy of the Visitation in Georgetown and became a favorite of President James Polk and his wife, Sarah, who were childless and also from Tennessee. Martha Johnson Patterson knew the White House well from her many visits with the Polks, but she was in no way the kind of grand hostess Priscilla Tyler had been. At her first social event while serving as her father's hostess, she told the guests, "We are plain people from the mountains of Tennessee, called here for a short time by a calamity. I trust not too much will be expected of us."

Her reference to Lincoln's assassination

as a calamity, even though it had made her father president, was not lost on Washington, nor was the humility and dignity of her tone. Her husband, David Patterson, was the junior senator from Tennessee, and she was well educated, but she put on no airs whatsoever, and she became highly regarded in a Washington torn by Reconstruction politics and the attempt to impeach her father. Her presence in the White House, with her husband and two children, and that of her widowed sister, Mary, and her three children, were Andrew Johnson's greatest bulwarks against despair in a very troubled time.

While Martha Patterson simply accepted the job of substitute First Lady as a necessary duty, not all presidential daughters were happy with such a situation. Perhaps the least enthralled of any by the idea of acting as White House hostess was Woodrow Wilson's daughter Margaret. She was the oldest of Ellen and Woodrow Wilson's three daughters and was twenty-eight when her mother died in August of 1914. The Wilsons had been an extremely close family, and her father was devastated by the loss of his wife. His two younger daughters, Jessie and Nell, had been married at the White House in November of 1913 and

May of 1914, so Margaret was seemingly the most logical choice to act as her father's hostess. But she was independent minded and had a flourishing career as a professional musician, so the job of substitute first lady was not something she relished. Yet she was actually the most outgoing and publicly assured of the three sisters and better equipped to handle the job than either Jessie or Nell would have been. She gritted her teeth and did the job so well that she became widely admired in Washington for her finesse in handling a difficult situation. Guests were particularly charmed by her after-dinner musical performances in the Blue Room or, for large groups, in the East Room. She played and sang beautifully, and even though she performed in part to avoid having to engage in what she regarded as trivial conversation, she added considerable brightness to a White House shadowed by her mother's death and the ongoing war in Europe. Nevertheless, Margaret was all too glad to give up her duties when her father married Edith Galt, a Washington widow, in December of 1915. She was not particularly fond of her stepmother, but now twenty-nine, Margaret was more than happy to escape the White House.

To be a true kid in the White House —

that is, under eighteen — can be a great delight, bringing treasured memories of what Jesse Grant called "the best playground in the world." White House parties for children have a special aura that stays with the youngsters of presidents for rest of their lives. But while grown children may be grateful for the opportunity to have lived in the President's House, they are quite often glad to be free of its special pressures and able to pursue their lives in their own way.

4

⧸∾⧹

White House Weddings

The public view of White House weddings has been shaped by the general media frenzy surrounding the marriages of President Lyndon Johnson's daughters Luci and Lynda Bird, and of President Richard Nixon's daughter Tricia. But the first two weddings to take place in the White House were of a very different nature. Both were low-key affairs, and both were marred by disputes between presidential children.

Maria Monroe was the first White House kid to be married in the President's House. She was fourteen when her father, James Monroe, took office in 1817 and only sixteen at the time of her marriage to twenty-one-year-old Samuel Lawrence Gouverneur in 1819. Today marriage at such a young age would be considered a scandal, but it was hardly unusual in the early nineteenth century. The groom came from a distinguished family, and the marriage had the complete blessing of James and Elizabeth Monroe. Unfortunately, the wedding plans were in the hands of Maria's older sister, Eliza.

Their mother, Elizabeth, had almost nothing to do with social events at the White House during her husband's two terms as president. Many in Washington believed that she was simply too haughty to involve herself with entertaining people whom she did not consider her equals, but there are also suggestions that she was ill. There is no more shadowy first lady in history, although in her earlier years she had been regarded as a woman of remarkable strength. When her husband was ambassador to France during the French Revolution in the 1790s, Elizabeth Monroe had personally intervened to secure the release from French prison of the wife of the Marquis de Lafayette, who had played such a prominent role in America's own Revolutionary War. But by the time she reached the White House twenty years later, Elizabeth had become a reclusive figure. Her elder daughter, Eliza, in her midtwenties and with a seven-year-old daughter of her own named Hortensia, served as hostess in her stead.

This arrangement did not make for many

festive White House occasions. Eliza was stern, humorless, and extremely tight with money, even when it was being provided by the White House budget. She regarded her lively younger sister, ten years her junior, as spoiled and frivolous and apparently did not approve of her marriage. Eliza invited a mere thirty guests to the wedding, ignoring the existence of Washington's diplomatic community as well as most members of Congress. The invitations that did go out were hurriedly printed at the last moment, even though the wedding had been planned for months, and the press was able to obtain no information except an extremely terse marriage announcement. The press, and the uninvited ambassadors and politicians, were furious, but Maria Monroe was the angriest of all and never forgave her older sister. Curiously, James Monroe's popularity was so great in this period — known as the Era of Good Feeling — that he was reelected without opposition the following year. Only one elector from New Hampshire cast a vote against him, giving it to John Quincy Adams of Monroe's own party, just to insure that only George Washington would have the honor of having been elected unanimously. In contrast, Maria Monroe harbored anything but good feelings toward her sister Eliza.

The next White House wedding was, if anything, an even stranger occasion. To begin with, it was the only White House wedding ever to be given for a president's son, breaking with the tradition of having the bride's family take responsibility for the ceremony. And in this case, too, friction between siblings was much in evidence.

The Adams family was known for its troubled family relationships. Two of John Quincy Adams's brothers had died — one of alcoholism — while their father, John Adams, was serving as the nation's second president, and his own three children — George, John, and Charles — had been raised under peculiar circumstances. In 1809 John Quincy Adams had been named ambassador to Russia by President James Madison. His wife, Louisa, accompanied him to Russia, bringing along two-year-old Charlie but leaving the older boys, George and John, in Massachusetts with their grandparents, former President John Adams and his wife, Abigail, who had also found themselves raising the boys' cousin, the famously ill-tempered Susannah.

John Quincy Adams didn't return from Europe with his wife and youngest son until 1817, so the two older boys were complete strangers to Charlie. Even so, he attached himself to George, the eldest, rather than to John, only two years his senior.

John was serving as his father's secretary at the White House when he was married in 1828, having been awarded that position when he, along with his entire senior class, had been expelled from Harvard for rioting about college rules. John's bride was Mary Catherine Hellen, and that caused a family schism since she had previously been engaged to his older brother, George. George refused to attend the wedding, and Charlie followed suit. Thus the second White House wedding, like the first, was a small private affair with an undercurrent of family tension.

The next White House wedding of a president's child didn't take place until forty-six years later, but it made up for the lapse in time by its opulence. Nellie Grant's nuptials were considered by the press at the time to be the most lavish event ever held in the White House. Ulysses S. Grant and his wife, Julia, one of the most affectionate couples ever to inhabit the White House, had allowed their sixteen-year-old daughter to travel to Europe in 1872 with family friend Adolph E. Borrie and his wife. Borrie, a very wealthy man who had briefly served as

Grant's secretary of the navy, showed young Nellie a very exciting time in Europe, and as a president's daughter she got to meet royalty, including Queen Victoria, and was widely entertained. On her return voyage to the United States, she met a young Englishman named Algernon Sartoris (pronounced "Sartress") and fell in love.

In his biography of Grant, William McFeely writes that Algernon's family "was not of very ancient lineage and limited distinction, but had an eye for acquisition. The Sartorises already owned one of the great ornaments of nineteenth-century England — Adelaide Kemble, Algernon's mother." Adelaide was the sister of the great actress Fanny Kemble and had been a major opera singer herself before her marriage. To the Grants, people of rather humble background, Algernon Sartoris looked like a real "catch" and a splendid match for their beloved Nellie, although the President was unhappy that she would be going to live in England. The Grants weren't sophisticated enough to realize that from the Sartorises' point of view, Nellie — as the daughter of America's greatest Civil War hero and a sitting president — was the real catch.

Several hundred guests were invited to Nellie's wedding on May 21, 1874. The

East Room had recently been redecorated in a very ornate style that some referred to disparagingly as "steamboat palace style" — and photographs from the period do suggest that it might well have been a room aboard a Mississippi gambling boat. The lush potted plants were augmented with huge bouquets of orange blossoms brought all the way up from Florida for the wedding. For weeks beforehand, the newspapers seemed to be covering little but the impending nuptials. The Marine Band provided the music, and Nellie was married on a special dais that was overhung with a huge bell constructed of white roses.

The marriage turned out to be a disaster. Algernon was certainly a philanderer and may have been an alcoholic, as well. And Nellie, bright and pretty as she was, found herself completely out of her depth in the social circle presided over by Adelaide Sartoris, one of the most brilliant conversationalists of the late Victorian age. William McFeeley suggests that in her very American kind of innocence, Nellie Grant might almost have been a model for Henry James's tragic heroine Daisy Miller. James in fact met Nellie and wrote of the encounter: "Meanwhile poor little Nellie Grant sits speechless on the sofa, understanding neither head nor tail of such high discourse and exciting one's compassion for her incongruous lot in life. She is as sweet and amiable as she is uncultivated — which is saying an immense deal." Although Nellie bore Algernon four children, she finally divorced him and returned to the United States after sixteen years of marriage. She married a Chicago businessman, Frank Hatch Jones, in 1912 and died in 1922 after a long illness.

Alice Roosevelt would have the next grand White House wedding in 1906. During four and half years in the White House, Alice had matured from a mischievous girl known for her attachment to her pet garter snake, Emily Spinach, to a striking beauty who had been entrusted by her father with goodwill trips to Latin America, China, and Japan. She probably received more press attention than any other president's child in the history of the White House. The American public was fascinated by her every utterance and fixated on her apparently vast wardrobe, although she always maintained that its size was largely the result of the numerous times she had been a bridesmaid and her ability to accessorize her gowns in a way that made the same dress appear to be an entirely new outfit. She was particularly noted for her love of the color blue, and more than a dozen years after her marriage a song was written for the Broadway hit *Irene* in tribute to her. "Alice Blue Gown" sold hundreds of thousands of sheet music copies and became an American standard that still shows up on recordings devoted to old American favorites.

In later years Alice would become legendary for her astringent wit. She could be devastating about later presidents, saying, for example, that "Harding was not a bad man. He was just a slob." While she denied that she had originated the famous remark about Calvin Coolidge looking as if "he had been weaned on a pickle," she freely admitted that she had done her best to spread it around. She could be shockingly frank about the facts of life, stating that having a baby was "like pushing a piano through a transom" window. And in her eighties and nineties, still entertaining an endless stream of the famous and the powerful in the drawing room of her Washington mansion, she had a pillow on which were embroidered the words IF YOU CAN'T SAY ANYTHING GOOD ABOUT SOMEONE, SIT RIGHT HERE BY ME.

Even as a young woman, her high spirits

and sharp humor made some people wonder who could possibly cope with her as a wife. Her father had his eye out for any likely contenders for her hand, though. Teddy himself saw to it that she was introduced to her future husband, Nicholas Longworth, telling her, "There's a young new congressman coming in who might amuse you." The President had been a member of the Porcellian Club when he attended Harvard, and since Nick Longworth had been, too, he seemed to Teddy a good prospect. Alice, to her surprise, found Nick delightful, and their engagement was soon announced. While Alice would have preferred to be married at Sagamore Hill, the family estate on Long Island, her father was not about to forgo the political advantages of having the first White House wedding since Nellie Grant's thirty-two years earlier.

Nellie Grant Sartoris, now fifty and long divorced, was one of the one thousand guests invited to the February 17, 1906, wedding. The ceremony was again held in the East Room, which had been redecorated in 1902 in a far simpler style and was adorned for the occasion by only a few flower arrangements. Alice had no attendants and simply entered the room on her father's arm to stand before the temporary altar. Her most vivid memory of the day was the sight of her three brothers standing at the bottom of the staircase with "their hair slicked back," smirking at her.

In *Mrs. L.*, the book by Michael Teague that recorded dozens of conversations he had with Alice Roosevelt Longworth seventy-five years later, when she was in her nineties but as sharp as ever, she recalled the wedding presents she had received:

Like everything else, they were exaggerated by the press, but nevertheless they still gave greedy me a good deal of pleasure. When I was asked what I wanted as presents, I said, "Trinkets, preferably diamond *trinkets." I particularly like the beautiful gold snuffbox from Edward VII with his miniature crest set in diamonds in the lid. I still have that. And then there was a beautiful Gobelin tapestry from the French government, a bracelet with diamonds (smaller than those he gave me when I christened his yacht, the* Meteor*) from the Kaiser, a rather hideous mosaic table from the King of Italy, and some really beautiful bolts of brocade from the dowager Empress of China that kept me regally clad in the evening for decades.*

Alice had, of course, met all of these royal

personages on various trips representing her father.

Her favorite gift was a set of pearls from Boucheron in Paris, which she wore throughout her life. That was a gift from Cuba, where her father had become a hero in 1898, leading the Rough Riders at the Battle of San Juan Hill. Teddy Roosevelt had been elected governor of New York that same year and was chosen as William McKinley's vice president in 1900. Alice and her husband even honeymooned in Cuba, where they made an excursion up the Rough Rider Trail. "We were accompanied by a mule laden down with refreshments, and I remember having a picnic by the side of the trail and being in a heated argument with Nick, about heaven knows what, under a tree."

Alice and Nick would have one daughter, Paulina. Nicholas Longworth rose to be Speaker of the House from 1925 until his sudden death in 1931 at the age of sixty. Alice, however, remained Washington's most famous hostess for another forty years. She knew every president from Benjamin Harrison to Ronald Reagan, a total of seventeen, and was an honored guest at the White House in every administration, whether Republican or Democratic. It has been said of her that since every president knew she would have a quotable opinion of them anyway, they might as well have her over to the White House in the hope of getting on her good side. Although she could be quite critical of the presidents themselves, she was always kind to their children (except possibly some of her Roosevelt cousins, the children of Franklin and Eleanor). Even sixty years after she lived in the White House, the Johnson and Nixon girls found her advice helpful — especially in terms of how to survive a White House wedding.

The White House logs that were kept about Alice Roosevelt's wedding were consulted in detail when two of Woodrow Wilson's daughters were married within six months of one another in 1913 and 1914. Woodrow and Edith Axson Wilson had three daughters. The eldest, Margaret, an accomplished professional musician like Margaret Truman three decades later, was twenty-six when her father became president. Jessie was twenty-five and Eleanor, called Nell, was twenty-three. Wilson had been a noted historian and president of Princeton University before being elected governor of New Jersey in 1910 and president in 1912. The family was regarded, therefore, as "bookish," which was not necessarily a compliment then any more than it is now. But although he could appear austere in public, Wilson had a puckish sense of humor in private. In her family memoir, Nell recalled that on the morning of his inauguration her father performed a little jig around her mother, singing, "We're going to the White House — today!"

The press immediately decided that having three unmarried presidential daughters wouldn't do and began linking them romantically to any man that they so much as said hello to. Fed up, Wilson told a press conference, "I am a public character . . . but the ladies of my household are not public characters because they are not servants of the government. I deeply resent the treatment they are receiving at the hands of the newspapers. . . . If this continues, I will deal with it not as President, but man to man." No newspaper published these words, but in that more circumspect age they actually seemed to have some effect — for a while.

But the press soon had an excuse to print a legion of personal stories about the Wilsons. In July of 1913, it was announced that Jessie was engaged to be married to Francis Bowes Sayre, an assistant district attorney in New York, and that the wedding would take place on November 25. Sayre seemed a good match for Jessie. He had accepted a position to teach at Williams College, which would take the Wilsons' middle daughter back to the kind of academic setting in which she had grown up. But in a way this wedding was somewhat traumatic for the family — and would have been if either of the other sisters had been the first to marry. They were all so close that it meant something would now be missing in the future. One of them would be gone most of the time.

Jessie's wedding was a grand affair, modeled on Alice Roosevelt's, with an even larger guest list, numbering several thousand. William Seale writes, "Blonde and angelic-looking, the bride wore white satin with a long train and veil. The bridesmaids wore silk in as many different shades of rose as there were bridesmaids. The dresses had short trains with a bit of silk-stockinged shin showing in front. Silver lace wired into high Russian-style crowns framed their faces." The country loved it — perhaps the Wilsons were something more than bookish after all.

In her book, *My Thirty Years Backstairs at the White House*, Lillian Rogers Parks gives a taste of the preparations for a White House wedding:

Everyone in the kitchen held their breath to keep from disturbing the cake, which was being baked by the same woman who had made the wedding cake for Alice Roosevelt when she married Representative Nicholas Longworth. Her name was Mme. Blanche Rales, and she came from New York just to bake the cake in the White House kitchen. The cake stood thirty inches high, and was three feet across and weighed 130 pounds. All the servants tiptoed by, afraid it would collapse.

No state dinner or other White House social event even begins to put as much strain on White House staff as the wedding of a president's daughter. Mrs. Parks and the other members of the staff were thus stunned to learn that Jessie's November 1913 wedding would be followed by the marriage of Nell in May 1914. The groom was William Gibbs McAdoo, the secretary of the treasury. Now the press really had something to talk about. McAdoo was twenty-six years older than Nell, a widower with two teenage children. Nell would admit that even her parents were none too thrilled with this match, but Nell herself was the most open, fun-loving, and least private of the Wilsons, and she took the noise in the press in stride. McAdoo didn't care — he adored Nell, and the marriage turned out to be a good one.

Nevertheless, a much smaller wedding was planned for May 7, 1914, which relieved the pressure on the White House staff and was in keeping with the fact that the groom had been married before. The number of guests was still in the low hundreds, however, large enough so that the hysterical sobs of the groom's oldest daughter, Nona, then in her midteens, went almost unnoticed as she broke down at the sound of the wedding march. Relatives quickly escorted her out of the Blue Room, and she was taken upstairs to regain her composure. The press didn't know about this disruption. But reporters and photographers were encamped all around the White House, waiting for the bride and groom to leave for their honeymoon. They were facing seasoned troops, however. The weddings of Alice Roosevelt and Jessie Wilson had led to more and more sophisticated ruses designed to facilitate an unobserved escape from the White House. In this case, after the reception, a whole series of cars pulled up at various White House exits. Each car seemed to be entered by the newlyweds, and photographers and reporters peeled off to follow them. Nell and her new husband eventually left quietly and unobserved. There would not be another president's daughter married in the White House for more than fifty years. But when the time came, Luci Baines Johnson would learn everything she could about how the three White House brides of the early years of the century had gone about "escaping" the White House following their marriages.

5

⌒

Shadows and Sorrows

To reach the White House is to achieve the pinnacle of power and success in America. But many presidents who have entered the mansion in triumph have left in bitterness and defeat, and even many of those who have been successful politically have endured great sadness while occupying the President's House. Others have not survived to complete their terms. William Henry Harrison, Zachary Taylor, and Warren Harding died of natural causes while serving as president; Abraham Lincoln, William McKinley, James Garfield, and John F. Kennedy were assassinated. A number of first ladies, particularly during the nineteenth century, were chronically ill, and Letitia Tyler and Ellen Wilson both died during their husband's terms.

The children of presidents who have died

in office have usually been adults at the time of their father's death. But Tad Lincoln, as we have seen, suffered not only the dreadful loss of his protective older brother Willie but also the assassination of his father; he would die of tuberculosis himself at the age of eighteen in 1871. Sixteen years later, the young sons of James A. Garfield, the last of the "log cabin" presidents born on the American frontier, found themselves facing the kind of horror that Tad Lincoln had in 1865 when his father was shot by John Wilkes Booth at Ford's Theater. Ironically, the person who gave Garfield's sons the greatest emotional comfort in their time of trial was Abraham Lincoln's only surviving son, Robert, who was serving as secretary of war in Garfield's cabinet.

James Garfield, despite his humble background, was a brilliant student who graduated from Williams College in 1856 and became a classics professor at Ohio's Hiram College and then its president. He also found time to become a lawyer. Only thirty when the Civil War broke out, he became the youngest general in the Union Army, and after his heroic conduct at the Battle of Chickamauga he was elected to Congress as a Republican representative in 1864. He became minority leader in 1876 and in 1880 was chosen as the Republican presidential candidate. He was a political supporter and close friend of the incumbent president, Rutherford B. Hayes, who was greatly delighted by his victory. So close were the two families that, uniquely in the history of the presidency, Hayes invited Garfield and his family to stay at the White House itself during the two weeks preceding Garfield's inauguration.

James and Lucretia Garfield had five children when he became president. The four sons were Harry, seventeen; Jim, fifteen; Irvin, ten; and Abram, eight. Daughter Mollie was fourteen. Fanny and Scott Hayes were nearly the same age as Mollie and Irvin Garfield, and during the two weeks prior to Garfield's inauguration, the children of the outgoing and incoming presidents of the United States could be seen playing together on the White House lawn in the snow.

But that happy domestic scene was in stark contrast to the turmoil to come. Shortly after the inauguration, Mrs. Garfield became extremely ill and nearly died. When she was strong enough, she went to their home on the New Jersey shore for the summer to continue her recuperation, taking the three younger children with her.

Harry and Jim remained at the White House with their father. All three were to join the rest of the family at the shore on July 2. On the appointed morning, they left for Washington's Baltimore and Potomac Railroad Station. There, a disappointed office seeker named Charles Julius Guiteau, who had tried several times to see the President without success, shot President Garfield in front of his teenage sons.

Secretary of War Robert Todd Lincoln put the local military units on immediate alert, suspecting the kind of conspiracy that had surrounded his own father's assassination. But it turned out that Guiteau was a deranged "lone gunman" who had operated entirely on his own. Garfield was brought back to the White House in a makeshift ambulance, the progress of which was impeded by hundreds of distraught citizens swarming the streets. The President had been struck by two bullets. One had struck him in the arm, but another was lodged in his spine. He was lucid but in great pain. As doctors arrived in large numbers at the White House, his sons stood near their father's bed in shock. Jim was weeping uncontrollably. Harry tried to console his younger brother without breaking into tears himself. Downstairs at the White House, Robert

Lincoln arrived and stood in the main hallway, weeping himself. He was heard to say, "How many hours of sorrow have I witnessed in this town."

Mrs. Garfield, despite her own weak condition, returned immediately to the White House and made heroic efforts to bolster her husband's spirits. Robert Lincoln tried to give solace to Harry and Jim, but he had been at Harvard when his own father was shot, and it had been Abe Lincoln's beloved little Tad who had been brought to his bedside to try to get through to his comatose father. Abraham Lincoln had died within a few hours, but Garfield survived for weeks. His children spent most of their time in their rooms, where the servants could often hear them weeping.

Numerous attempts were made to extract the bullet from Garfield's spine, none of them successful. Even Alexander Graham Bell tried to use an electronic device to pinpoint the exact location of the bullet. Ironically, in 1876 Bell had demonstrated his new invention, the telephone, to President-elect Hayes, who had commented, "That's an amazing invention, but who would ever want to use one of them?" Now Robert Todd Lincoln had been informed of Garfield's shooting by telephone, and the inventor himself had been brought in to try to help save the life of Hayes's great good friend and successor.

The White House in those days was like an oven in summer. The heat was particularly hard on the President, and several eminent scientists worked urgently to try to rig up a cooling system that would alleviate his suffering. They finally managed by trial and error, using hoses that ran from the basement through holes punched in the White House walls and floors, to contrive an apparatus that actually worked. The principles of what would become known as air-conditioning were first discovered in the White House that dreadful summer as President Garfield lay dying.

In September, at Garfield's request, it was agreed that he would be moved to Long Branch, New Jersey, to the house by the sea where he had been headed with Harry and Jim on the day he was shot two months earlier. There, surrounded by his family, he died on September 19, 1881. It was exactly the eighteenth anniversary of his victory over the Confederate forces at Chickamauga in 1863, a battle that had begun to turn the tide for the Union forces, made him a hero, and been the basis of his entry into politics. His body would lie in state in Washington but not in the East Room of the White House, as Lincoln's had. Instead, he was placed in the rotunda of the Capitol, where he had served for fifteen years as a representative from Ohio.

Garfield's children, who had perhaps experienced real happiness at the White House only when they played in the snow with the Hayes children before their father became president, nevertheless survived the trauma of his death to lead more successful and pleasant lives than many White House kids. Mollie would eventually marry Joe Brown, her father's very young and devoted secretary, who had dealt superbly with the press during her father's death watch. She and Joe had a double ceremony with her brother Harry and his bride. Harry, Jim, and Irvin all became attorneys, while young Abram, who carried his father's middle name as his first name, became an architect.

On August 2, 1923, the two sons of Vice President Calvin Coolidge left their grandfather's home in Plymouth Notch, Vermont, to take summer jobs. Although Calvin Coolidge had developed his political career in Massachusetts, the family returned whenever possible to Plymouth Notch, where he had grown up. Young John Coolidge, born

September 7, 1906, and Calvin Jr., born April 13, 1908, would not learn until the next day that they were now the sons of the President of the United States. Warren G. Harding had died of a heart attack in a San Francisco hospital, where he had been recovering from pneumonia contracted on a grueling trip to Alaska. There wasn't even a telephone in the house at Plymouth Notch, and Calvin Coolidge had been sworn in as president by his own father, a notary public, in the dim light of kerosene lamps at 2:47 A.M.

While their father and their mother, Grace, returned to Washington, the two boys continued their summer jobs. There was no question of their doing anything else. Calvin Jr.'s job that summer was to harvest tobacco leaves, and when another worker said to him that if *his* father were president, *he* certainly wouldn't be working in a tobacco field, fifteen-year-old Cal replied, "If my father were your father, you would." When Cal did join his parents at the White House, he discovered that there was a lot of mail for him, as there was for John. One letter to Cal, from a boy his own age, addressed him as "the first boy of the land." Young Cal replied, "I think you are mistaken in calling me the first boy of the land, since I have done nothing. It is my father who is President. Rather, the first boy of the land would be some boy who had distinguished himself through his own actions."

Both Coolidge boys were modest and well behaved. Unlike Tad and Willie Lincoln or Teddy Roosevelt's sons, they were not cutups. Both attended Mercersberg Academy, a boarding school in New Jersey less than two hours from Washington, so that they were often at the White House even when it wasn't a regular vacation period. John and Cal Jr. were very close despite a considerable difference in their personalities, with John echoing his father's seriousness and Cal, his mother's gift for merriment. It should be noted, however, that despite President Coolidge's reserved public demeanor, he had a considerable dry wit and, somewhat surprisingly, was given to teasing his sons. John didn't take this too well, although Cal Jr. seemed to thrive on it. Grace Coolidge would later write that her husband "could never get a great deal of satisfaction out of teasing Calvin, for his younger son entered into the spirit of it and enjoyed the encounter even more than his father did, but John was a more shy and sensitive child, and I could never get him to understand or adopt Calvin's method of outwitting his father. Occasionally John and I managed to turn the tables on him."

John would later say that the best thing about living in the White House was that he and his brother got to ride horses whenever they wanted to. They also played a lot of tennis on the White House courts. Cal was particularly good at it and often invited friends over to play. Then one day in June of 1924 he developed a blister after playing in sneakers without socks. He bathed the blister and put iodine on it, but within a couple of days he had become extremely listless. Mrs. Coolidge asked the White House physician, Dr. Joel Boone, to take a look at her son. Admiral Boone was immediately alarmed, took blood samples, and delivered them to Walter Reed Hospital for analysis. It turned out that the blister had become infected, and because Cal had stoically ignored the problem, it had become very serious. (Penicillin had not yet been discovered — and even then it would not become available until a crash program at the start of World War II.) July 4 was Coolidge's fifty-second birthday — a birth date he shared with Thomas Jefferson and John Adams — but it proved to be the worst he had ever spent. By now the entire nation knew that Cal Jr. was gravely ill. Bulletins were even read at the Democratic convention in New York, which had assembled to choose a candidate to face President Coolidge in the fall election.

An operation was performed on Cal at Walter Reed, and every possible technique then available was tried, including saline injections and blood transfusions. But it was clear to almost everyone that the youth could not survive. Even former President William Howard Taft, now the chief justice of the United States, wrote to his wife saying that Cal was on his deathbed and that the whole country was there with him. Cal was often delirious, but the night of July 6 he was able to whisper to his parents, "Good night, Father and Mother. Don't worry anymore." The next night he seemed to imagine in his fever that he was leading troops in battle. But then, as his father would later say, "He must have had some premonition, some intimation, for suddenly his body seemed to relax and he murmured 'We surrender.'" Admiral Boone exclaimed, "No, Calvin, never surrender!" But the sixteen-year-old had lapsed into a coma from which he wouldn't awake.

Calvin Coolidge Jr. was the first child to die in the White House since Abraham and Mary Lincoln's son Willie at the height of the Civil War. Back then the nation had been torn in half, and boys still in their teens were dying in battle daily. Now, though, the nation was at peace, and the country opened its heart to the Coolidges. There was considerable public weeping as parents were reminded of sons they had lost all too recently in World War I, many to rampant infections like Calvin's that, in the absence of penicillin, had proved far more deadly than their actual battle wounds.

Calvin's casket was placed in the East Room, with a guard of honor, and a service was held there on July 9th. His body was taken that night to Northampton, Massachusetts, where he had spent his childhood, accompanied on a special train by his family and several cabinet members. There, another service was held. Grace Coolidge biographer Ishbel Ross writes, "Children lined the entire route . . . to the church. . . . The Smith College chimes rang out and mothers who had gone shopping or baby-walking with Mrs. Coolidge stood on the sidelines and watched her with sympathy." Calvin was then taken to Plymouth Notch to be buried in the small cemetery there, in what Grace Coolidge, describing the burial in a letter to her friend Mrs. Reuben B. Hills, called "God's acre . . . I remembered

Calvin as I saw him last in that hallowed place helping his Grandfather cut the grass and rake it, hardly more than a year before. Yes, he did love Plymouth, even as a little fellow when he was out on a rise of ground in the morning with his Grandfather and looking around said, 'This is a great place, Grandfather.'"

Despite Calvin Coolidge's nomination and election in his own right that year, political victory could not compensate for the loss of the Coolidges' younger son. The presidency is so pressured and event-filled that Calvin and Grace Coolidge were able to go forward with at least a public display of fortitude. But the White House would never be the same to John. During his father's full second term, he was attending Amherst College, and although he kept in close touch with his parents and came to Washington for major holidays, such visits reminded him all too deeply of his brother's absence.

In the summer of 1929, after the Coolidges had left the White House, Grace was able at last to give full vent to her feelings about the loss of her son. On the fifth anniversary of young Calvin's death, she wrote a poem that was published in *Good Housekeeping* to wide interest and sympathy. The $250 check she received for it she gave to John just before his wedding at the end of that summer to Florence Trumbull, the daughter of the governor of Connecticut, telling him to buy something for his new house with it. Grace Coolidge's poem was called "The Open Door."

You, my son
Have shown me God.
Your kiss upon my cheek
Has made me feel the gentle touch
Of him who leads us on.
The memory of your smile, when young
Reveals His face,
As mellowing years come on apace.
And when you went before,
You left the fates of Heaven ajar
That I might glimpse,
Approaching from afar,
The glories of his Grace.
Hold, Son, my hand,
Guide me along the path,
That, coming,
I may stumble not,
Nor roam,
Nor fail to show the way
Which leads us — Home.

PART II

∾

1944–1998

IN THE MEDIA AGE

∾

6

∽

The Trumans and Eisenhowers

A few minutes after 5:30 on the afternoon of April 12, 1945, Harry Truman made a telephone call from the president's office in the West Wing of the White House. At the other end of the line, his daughter, Margaret, picked up the phone in the vice president's residence. She started to tease him about being late for dinner, but he cut her off quickly, asking to speak to her mother, Bess Truman. Margaret, the Trumans' only child, whom her father doted on, was annoyed, but she quickly discovered the reason for her father's uncustomarily abrupt tone with her. Just a few minutes earlier, after being asked to come immediately to the White House from the Capitol, he had been informed in the family quarters by First Lady Eleanor Roosevelt that her husband, Franklin, the President of the United States, had died that afternoon at the Roosevelts' vacation home in Warm Springs, Georgia. A stunned Harry Truman realized that he himself had been president for over an hour without realizing it. He had the presence of mind to ask Mrs. Roosevelt if there was anything that he could do for her. Eleanor Roosevelt, after more than twelve years as first lady, knew the weight that was about to fall on Harry Truman's shoulders and turned the question around. Addressing him as Mr. President, she asked quietly if there was anything that she could do for him.

Margaret Truman, born February 7, 1924, was twenty-one years old and in her third year at George Washington University in the nation's capital. On hearing the news from her mother, she changed out of the dress she had put on for a date and into a more suitable one, then accompanied her mother to the White House, where her father was sworn in as the country's thirty-third president just after seven o'clock by Chief Justice Harlan F. Stone, who had originally been appointed an associate justice by Calvin Coolidge in 1925 and named chief justice by Roosevelt in 1941.

Margaret Truman was extremely proud of her father and firmly believed that due to Franklin Roosevelt's foresight, the country had the best possible new leader. But neither she nor her mother were taken with the White House. The public rooms looked reasonably well kept, but she was to comment that the private quarters more closely resembled a third-rate boardinghouse. It was only in the first year of her father's presidency that she really lived in the White House. Her mother, who had never liked Washington, preferred to spend as much time as possible at the family home in Independence, Missouri, and Margaret spent some time there with her. But she was already a young woman, and in the fall of 1946 her primary place of residence became New York City, where she studied singing, first with the Metropolitan Opera star Helen Traubel (who had been born and raised back in St. Louis, Missouri, on Truman home turf) and later with a noted New York coach, Sidney Dietch.

Moreover, not even Margaret's parents lived in the White House for a major part of Truman's presidency. It was not merely the shabbiness of the personal quarters that was a problem; the entire structure was in danger of collapsing. This was partially due to the fact that it was a very old house, although its soundness had been further compromised when President Coolidge had the roof raised — the only time the taciturn Republican had ever "raised the roof," Harry Truman liked to say — to turn the third floor from storage rooms into additional quarters for the first family. That renovation had used so much cement, it gradually compromised the floors below. It was Margaret Truman who first discovered how bad the situation was. One of the legs of her spinet piano went through the floor, and the ceiling broke open in the State Room beneath. A complete structural examination of the house was done, and Commissioner of Public Buildings W. E. Reynolds concluded that the second floor was "staying up there purely from habit." That led to a massive renovation that involved an almost complete gutting of the White House, and the Trumans spent nearly three years living in Blair House across the street.

Although Margaret spent only brief periods of time in Washington, she was more in the news than any president's daughter since Alice Roosevelt. Her singing career was launched with a national tour that got her on the front pages of newspapers across the country. While the tour was a financial success, Margaret's singing sometimes got rather carping reviews. Harry Truman didn't like seeing his beloved daughter criticized, but he kept his mouth shut until a particularly mean review in the *Washington Post* caused him to lose his temper.

The President wrote a letter to critic Paul Hume, saying, "I've just read your lousy review of Margaret's concert. . . . I've come to the conclusion that you are an 'eight-ulcer man on four-ulcer pay.' " Much as the public liked Margaret, many people thought her father was out of line, and Margaret at least gave the impression that she wished he had kept quiet. For a time she continued to tour, but she eventually concentrated more on radio and television appearances that "highbrow" critics paid less attention to. She also began to appear as an actress in summer stock with considerable success. While Margaret was no beauty, she had an attractive personality, a good figure, a winning smile, and the ability to charm audiences. There was little doubt that many people went to her concerts and stage appearances because she was the President's daughter, but she was also an accomplished professional, and few patrons went away feeling shortchanged.

Nearly four years after her father left the White House, Margaret married a *New York Times* editor, Clifton Daniel. They had four sons, but in addition to raising a family,

Margaret forged an entirely new career for herself as a writer. She started out with a 1969 book on the history of White House pets. Her 1973 biography of her father, published a few months after his death, became a major best-seller and is regarded as one of the most accomplished modern works by a member of a first family. She then turned her attention to fiction and has had great success with her series of mystery novels set in Washington, D.C., which regularly make the best-seller lists. The biggest seller of all had a title that this accomplished daughter of a United States president must have found irresistible: *Murder at the White House.*

The television age began during the Truman years. He was the first person to give a nationally televised speech, broadcast from San Francisco in late 1945 at the conclusion of the international conference that drew up the United Nations Charter. He subsequently became the first president to speak to the nation from the Oval Office and the first to hold a televised news conference. There had been very few television sets at the time to receive his San Francisco speech, but by the end of his term, in January of 1953, television was already established as the most influential communications medium the world had ever known. The political conventions were televised for the first time in 1952, and during Dwight Eisenhower's two terms, the medium came to dominate both news and entertainment.

The rise of television had an enormous effect on political life, but it also deeply affected the way all subsequent first families led their public and private lives. White House kids were as much affected by the new medium as their parents. Privacy had always been difficult to come by in the White House. Since the 1880s photographers had been at the ready to snap a picture of anyone who ventured onto the White House lawn. Television cameras were even more intrusive, and the days of White House kids wandering out on their own accord to play on the South Lawn were gone forever. New plantings on the White House grounds shielded some small areas from prying electronic eyes, but to a large extent the children of presidents were forced to stay indoors at the White House. And when older children made trips to other parts of the country, they had to be constantly aware that a television camera might be trained on them at any time, particularly as lighter, more mobile units were developed.

Television also increased public interest in the private lives of first families, including the children, which had both beneficial and harmful effects. While public affection for toddlers, like the Eisenhower grandchildren and the Kennedy kids, certainly helped to create a sense of connectedness with the men who were the fathers or grandfathers of these youngsters, it could backfire with older children, whose every public appearance could be scrutinized by a hundred million viewers for signs of arrogance or misbehavior. The White House was less than ever a home and more a public stage for presidential offspring.

Margaret Truman was fully aware of this increased scrutiny, but she was a grown woman with a very public career of her own and took it in stride. And, fortunately for Ike and Mamie Eisenhower's grandchildren, they were still young enough so that public reaction to them consisted of "aren't they cute" rather than the "where did she get that awful dress" reactions that would later dog the Johnson and Nixon girls.

Eisenhower and his wife, Mamie, had had two sons, but the elder, Doud Dwight, called Ikky, had died of scarlet fever at the age of three. Their second son, John Sheldon Doud Eisenhower, born August 3, 1922, had attended West Point like his father, graduating on D-Day in 1944. At the time his father was elected president, John was serving as an officer of the Fifteenth Infantry in Korea, but his wife, Barbara, was living in Virginia with their three children — David, almost five years old; Barbara Anne (called Anne), three and a half years old; and Susan, less than a year old. Their fourth child, Mary Jean, would be born in December.

David, Anne, and Susan were frequent visitors to the White House and adored by their grandparents — perhaps all the more since Dwight and Mamie had lost a son when he was very young. With John Eisenhower away so much on military duty, the kids and their mother were encouraged to spend as much time as possible at the Executive Mansion. And when their father was home on leave, Ike and Mamie often took charge of their grandchildren to give John and Barbara some time to themselves. Thus some areas of the White House looked as though young children lived there all the time. In her memoir about her grandmother, *Mrs. Ike*, Susan Eisenhower recalls that Mamie had set aside a large room on the third floor as a playroom. The Solarium was set aside as a "sitting and dining room for us when we visited. Mamie kept three birds there for our enjoyment, a canary and two parakeets: Gabby, High Glory, and Pete. When Pete died, she allowed us to give him a solemn burial on the edge of what is now the Rose Garden."

David would subsequently recall that one of the pleasures of the White House playroom was that he could set up his toy soldiers there and simply leave them set up for as long as he liked, whereas at home he would have put them away after playing with them. There were also bicycles for all three children, which they were even allowed to ride in the ground-floor hallways when there were no tours or receptions in progress. David's particular joy was to drive around the White House in "an electric miniature of a Thunderbird," and the girls got to drive it, too. Mamie "also welcomed us into her room after her staff meetings," Susan remembers, "and we would rummage through the knick-knacks she kept for us on her side table. She could be a captivating grandmother; her shimmering blue eyes held you in their enchanting grip while she imparted secrets and planned conspiracies."

But Mamie was also a considerable disciplinarian:

No running up and down corridors, no sliding down bannisters, no greasy fingers on the woodwork, no getting down from the table before the meal was over. All of us were strictly schooled in manners, and Mamie even taught us to use finger bowls properly by the time we were three years old. We would receive admonitions about drying our hair after swimming in the White House pool, and lectures about wearing warm clothing when we went out to play — scolding about wet heads and inadequate clothing coming, perhaps, from her reflexive fear about our health and well-being.

Mamie Eisenhower obviously would not have put up with the wild antics of Tad and Willie Lincoln or Teddy Roosevelt's children.

But even with Mamie keeping them in line, the Eisenhower grandchildren clearly had a wonderful time at the White House. David, who was five when his grandfather became president and thirteen when Ike's two terms came to an end, had clearly developed a proprietary feeling about the President's House. He fully understood, of course, that the mansion did not belong to his grandfather and that he would be lucky to get to visit it at all with a new family of

Democrats taking up residence. But he wanted to leave his mark on the great house. On the last day he spent there just before President Kennedy's inauguration in January of 1961, David put down a few words on a piece of paper: "I will return." This message echoed the famous words of General Douglas MacArthur when Japan captured the Philippines during World War II. David Eisenhower took his message up to the third floor and hid it under a rug. And, like MacArthur, David did indeed return, eight years later — as the son-in-law of the man who had just been defeated by John F. Kennedy, Richard M. Nixon.

7

∽

Kennedy Kids

During the 1960 presidential campaign, President Dwight Eisenhower had called the supposedly inexperienced Democratic candidate, John F. Kennedy, a "whippersnapper." But the forty-four-year-old JFK quickly proved himself up to the job, and the only whippersnapper to be found in the White House was his son, John Fitzgerald Kennedy Jr., who got nicknamed John-John because his father always had to say his name twice before he came running. In fact, he wasn't even crawling when the family moved into the White House. Jackie Kennedy had been pregnant with him during the campaign. She had caused a lot of raised eyebrows when a reporter asked her an election-eve question about whether the baby would be born by inauguration day, and she had replied with her own question: "When is inauguration day?"

It would be a long time before the public fully understood Jackie's deadpan sense of humor and came to realize that this answer had been a putdown of a question she regarded as extremely dumb — she was all too obviously in her ninth month.

John Jr. was born on November 17, 1960, two weeks early. The Kennedys' daughter, Caroline, had been born November 27, 1957, and would be three years old when her father became president. The public had been amused and charmed by the Eisenhower grandchildren, but they were, after all, grandchildren and not even full-time White House residents. John Jr. and Caroline were the youngest children of a president since Grover Cleveland's seventy years earlier. The Clevelands had kept their children almost invisible. While Jackie knew she couldn't get away with that, she was determined to keep firm control of when and where her children would be photographed. As Christopher Andersen makes clear in his book *Jack and Jackie,* the issue of photographs was sometimes a matter of contention between the parents. The President, who was aware of the fact that his adorable kids were a political asset, and who also enjoyed seeing their pictures in newspapers and magazines, would occasionally authorize the release of photographs without telling the First Lady. When she blew her stack, he would pretend innocence, and various White House staffers would get saddled with the blame. Andersen quotes press secretary Pierre Salinger, Jackie's social secretary Tish Baldridge, and White House photographer and family friend Jacques Lowe about the problem. Salinger noted, "From the moment she set foot in the White House," Jackie wanted to keep the children "out of the spotlight." Baldridge commented that the children "*were* stars," even though Jackie didn't want them to be. Contrasting Jackie's paranoia about press photos of the children and Jack's desire to show them off, Lowe said, "It got to be a game between them, with me stuck in the middle."

In the end a number of photographs of the Kennedy children at the White House got published. The public was delighted to see Caroline astride her pony, Macaroni, but the most famous of all photographs of the Kennedy children was the one of John-John peeking out from under his father's desk, taken by *Look* magazine's Stanley Tretick. Even Jackie approved of this set of photos.

President Kennedy's desk had been discovered in the White House basement by Jackie herself, on one of her forays to find historic treasures to display in what she initially considered a very dowdy mansion. The desk had originally been presented to President Hayes by Queen Victoria and was constructed from timbers salvaged from the British warship HMS *Resolute*. Jackie had it refinished and put into the Oval Office as a surprise for her husband about a month after they moved in. John-John loved the desk because it had a hinged panel at the front that swung open like a door. Kenneth P. O'Donnell, JFK's close confidant, described the game that the President and his son played with the desk in his memoir *"Johnny, We Hardly Knew Ye"*:

> *John would hide under the desk while the President was talking to me and other staff members about the day's appointments. We would hear a scratching noise behind the panel of the desk, and the President would exclaim, "Is there a rabbit in there?" The panel would swing open and John would pop out of the desk, growling and then rolling on the carpet screaming with laughter.*

Photographer Stanley Tretick described

to Christopher Andersen another Oval Office scene. "His interest in the boy was incredible. It was almost sensual. John-John was sitting on the floor of the Oval Office one night and the President was talking to him. . . . And then he just kind of reached for him — he reached for the boy and pulled his pajama top up . . . and he kind of rubbed his bare skin right above his rear end. He wanted to touch him." This scene is reminiscent of Abraham Lincoln holding his son Tad on his lap, with his "long, bony hand" spread out over the boy's dark hair.

Both Caroline and John-John had the run of the White House much of the time, which meant that they were liable to pop up unexpectedly and sometimes at inopportune moments. Caroline once appeared on all fours between the President's legs during a press conference. Another time, dinner guests got out of the elevator to see her running naked down the hallway with her nanny, Maud Shaw, in hot pursuit. Not everything was fun and games, however. Jackie Kennedy had set up a school on the third floor for Caroline and nearly twenty other children of White House staffers and friends. But the President would often drop in on their lessons to say hello. Tish Baldridge has recalled, "The house was full of children morning, noon, and night. You never knew when an avalanche of young people would come bearing down on you, runny noses, dropped mittens in the hall, bicycles. . . ."

Even during moments of grave international crisis, President Kennedy had special time for his children. There have been dozens of books on the Cuban Missile Crisis, but Ken O'Donnell brought a unique perspective to it in his memoir, recalling how profoundly aware everyone in the White House was of the dreadful fate that untold numbers of children would face if the nuclear confrontation between the United States and the Soviet Union was not peacefully resolved.

O'Donnell relates the question his own wife asked him. "While you're safe with the President under a rock someplace," she said, "what am I supposed to do with your five children?" He goes on to tell how Dave Powers had joined the President that Saturday night in mid-October of 1962 for JFK's usual evening swim in the White House pool. Kennedy himself raised his concerns about children everywhere during that swim:

Later Dave went to the upstairs apartment in the mansion with a folder of reports the President wanted to study that night. Coming into the dimly lit living room to give the President the papers, Dave heard [JFK's] voice as he talked quietly and assumed that he was alone, speaking to somebody on the telephone. Then he saw the President sitting in a chair with Caroline on his lap, reading to her from a storybook.

"I watched him sitting there with Caroline," Dave said to me later. "I thought of what he had been saying to me in the pool, about how worried he was about the children everywhere in the world, and, you know, I got the strangest feeling. I handed him the papers, and got out of there as fast as I could. I was all choked up."

By the end of October, the crisis was over, and Caroline got a treat few White House kids have been allowed to experience. Such Washington luminaries as Arthur Schlesinger, Joe Alsop, and Dean Acheson answered the doorbells of their Georgetown homes to find still another contingent of Halloween witches and goblins calling out "Trick or treat!" But this group had something different about it. In the background was a woman, also masked, whose voice telling the children to say thank you was immediately recognizable as that of Jackie Kennedy. She and Caroline and the young friends who had come along on this outing were of course being discreetly protected by the Secret Service. Still, this was a daring excursion. The last White House kids who had been able to make such a Halloween outing were Teddy Roosevelt's children, more than fifty years earlier.

Jackie saw even more of the children than her husband did, in fact. The stories about the Kennedy kids tend to focus on the President's activities with them because the amount of time he spent in their company was remarkable for so busy a man. (Even Jackie was surprised and delighted at how much attention her husband gave to their children.) What's more, her time with them was private, out of sight of those who would go on to write memoirs of the Kennedy years. And neither she nor her children ever talked about the private details of the White House years with the press.

But it was Jackie who saw to it that the very first boxes of Kennedy belongings moved into the White House — and hidden in a closet by the chief usher, J. B. West, two weeks before the inauguration — were the children's toys. It was Jackie who oversaw the construction of a playground hidden by trees and bushes just outside the White House. There the White House carpenters constructed a barrel tunnel, a slide, a trampoline, a swing, a tree house, and even rabbit hutches. Jackie drew detailed sketches for each element.

Caroline's room was the only one that retained what Jackie disparaged as "Mamie pink" on its walls — a color that had been all over the White House. Caroline shared the room with her hamsters and her canary, Robin. Eventually one corner would be taken up with a very large, ornate dollhouse given to her by Charles de Gaulle — an edifice that Fanny Hayes would certainly have envied.

The Kennedy children loved animals, and there were two dogs, named Charlie and Pushinka, as well as lambs and ducks. Caroline's pony, Macaroni, had a special place in her affections, however. Leonard Bernstein recalled being at the White House and wanting to take a look at the first broadcast of one of his televised *Young People's Concerts*. He was ushered into Caroline's bedroom and watched with her and Maud Shaw. "I remember very well Caroline sitting, hypnotized, or so I thought, by this program and just thrilled with every moment. We were sitting holding hands, and she was all wrapped up in the concert, and then she suddenly looked up at me with this marvelous clear face and said, 'I have my own horse.' Now that really brought me down to earth, so at that moment I turned off the set and rejoined the others."

In the late spring of 1963, Caroline and John-John were told that they would have a baby brother or sister in the fall. But the child, Patrick, was born five weeks premature on August 7 and died of respiratory problems two days later. It was explained to Caroline and John that Patrick had gone to heaven. They accepted that, and their bereaved parents tried hard to conceal their own heartache. In his social history of mid-twentieth-century America, *The Glory and the Dream*, William Manchester describes how the president took John-John along to Veteran's Day ceremonies at Arlington National Cemetery on November 11, 1963:

To the indignation of some, who thought the occasion should be solemn, the little boy was allowed to toddle into the procession and disrupt it. His father was delighted, and while he beamed down at the child, cameramen put the scene on celluloid. There were those who thought that Kennedy had brought the boy along with that in mind. Look *was coming out with an exclusive spread of John Jr. pictures; it would have been like the President to stage something for photographers who would feel left out of it.*

But a nation that smiled at John-John's antics that day would be weeping just over two weeks later when President John Fitzgerald Kennedy was himself buried at Arlington following his assassination in Dallas, Texas, on November 22nd. The images of those late November days are burned into the memories of most Americans who were old enough to understand what was happening: the President recoiling from the shot that killed him, as captured on the scene by the Zapruder film; Lyndon Johnson being sworn in as president on *Air Force One* with a stunned Jackie Kennedy standing beside him; Jackie, still wearing her bloodstained pink suit the following day when she went to the Capitol where her husband lay in state; the murder of Lee Harvey Oswald, the presumed assassin, on live television by Jack Ruby.

But perhaps the image that retains the most emotional impact so many years later is John Fitzgerald Kennedy Jr., standing with his mother, his sister, and his uncle, Attorney General Robert Kennedy, as his father's coffin was borne down Pennsylvania Avenue in a funeral procession led by kings, presidents, and prime ministers, walking together with grim determination into an uncertain future. John-John's salute to his fallen father, small hand raised smartly in a final farewell, seemed all the more poignant because the photograph of him popping out from under his father's desk in the Oval Office had appeared in *Look* only two weeks earlier. John-John had turned three years old on November 17, five days before his father's murder.

Maud Shaw had been delegated to tell the children of their father's death before their mother returned to Washington with the President's body. She told them that their father had gone to look after Patrick. "Patrick was so lonely in heaven. He didn't know anyone there. Now he has the best friend anybody could have." Christopher Andersen reports, "[W]hen John-John was told, he asked, 'Did Daddy take his plane with him?' Miss Shaw said yes. 'I wonder,' the boy said, 'when he's coming back.'"

The little boy grew up into a man regarded as even more handsome than his father. He became a lawyer and founded *George*, a magazine of political commentary.

His older sister, Caroline, also took a law degree. She married artist Edwin Schlossberg in 1986, and they have three children, Rose, 9, Tatiana, 7, and John, 4. Jackie, it is widely agreed, raised her children well. Caroline does her best to lead a very private life, but John was always in the news, and his death in July 1999 created the kind of media circus that had attended the death of Princess Diana of Great Britain two years earlier. He was killed, along with his wife of three years, Caroline Bessette Kennedy, and his sister-in-law, when the plane he had recently bought and which he was piloting went down in the dark waters off Martha's Vineyard. When the news broke, the first thought in the minds of many Americans was inevitably of the small boy saluting his slain father's coffin thirty-six years earlier. No other White House kid has ever left a more indelible mark on the public memory.

8

⁓

The Johnson Girls

Lyndon Baines Johnson, like Harry Truman, became president of the United States with shocking suddenness, and like the Trumans, the Johnsons gave the president's widow ample time to recover from the shock and depart the White House. President Kennedy was assassinated on November 22, 1963, but it was not until Saturday, December 7, that the Johnsons began to occupy the executive mansion. There was no permanent vice presidential residence until Jimmy Carter's administration, when the vice presidential residence was first occupied by Vice President Walter F. Mondale and his family. Like so many vice presidential families before them, the Johnsons lived in their own home. It was called The Elms, and Johnson had bought it while he was the majority leader of the Senate. In many ways they were sad to leave it and put it up for sale. Lady Bird Johnson had worked hard to make it a lovely home, and it was the repository of many memories.

The Johnsons' daughters were, according to their mother, of two minds about what was happening. They were excited that their father was president but aware that their lives would become more complicated and far less private. Lynda Bird Johnson was the older daughter, born March 19, 1944, during her father's fourth term as a congressman from Texas. Luci Baines Johnson was born July 2, 1947; originally christened Lucy, she insisted on changing the spelling as a teenager. Their father was elected to the Senate in 1948 and had an extraordinarily rapid rise to power and influence, being elected majority leader in 1954. The Johnson girls had thus grown up in Washington — unlike the children of most presidents — although they also spent a lot of time at the family ranch on the Perdenales River in Texas. They were nineteen and sixteen when their father became president, Luci studying at Washington's National Cathedral School, Lynda a freshman at the University of Texas at Austin. Luci was at home at the White House all the time, while Lynda flew up from Texas on an almost weekly basis and was in Washington for most major White House events.

Both daughters were attractive, with black hair like their mother, but Luci was more vivacious and outgoing, Lynda more reserved and studious. Both could charm White House visitors as easily as their mother — all three had winning smiles — but Lynda also had the ability to hold her own in serious conversation with the likes of the economist Walter Heller, who was the head of the Council of Economic Advisers under President Kennedy and an adviser to President Johnson, and the architect Philip Johnson, who designed the New York State Theater at Manhattan's Lincoln Center for the Performing Arts, among many other important buildings. Thus both Luci and Lynda were called upon to play major roles in the heavy White House entertaining schedule, and either was capable of stepping in for their mother if the need arose. That would subsequently prove to be the case with the Nixon daughters, Tricia and Julie, as well, but the Johnson girls enjoyed campaigning far more than Tricia and Julie did, and they played a larger part in their father's political life.

Luci made herself so at home in the White House that her mother, as Lady Bird reports in her book *A White House Diary*, walked into the Treaty Room one day "and found Luci's algebra and Latin texts and some frayed notebooks and some chewed pencils lying there on that famous table. Obviously she had been doing her homework in the Treaty Room for several nights." In her diary, Lady Bird added, "I think I'd better put a stop to it. It's a little too much of a museum for that."

Lady Bird was more seriously concerned by Luci's determination to join the Catholic Church. The family was religious but had become nondenominational; like many political families, they tended to go to several different churches of various faiths in the course of any given year. Luci was not only the most religious member of the family, she seemed to need the greater certainties offered by Catholicism. By the fall of 1963 she had begun to take instruction. Lady Bird confided to her diary, "I feel a sense of separation, almost as though I were saying goodby to her. . . . And yet I have never seen her happier or more radiant, and I know that for her, religion is a very necessary, deep, and important part of life. This decision has been coming on for about five years — it is no flash in the pan — so I can't say no. How could I make it stick? How would I dare to presume I was right?"

131

Luci's best friend in Washington, Warrie Lynn Smith (who was also close to Lynda) was Catholic, but Lady Bird noted that she was no proselytizer and had advised Luci to take her time and make certain that she wanted to convert. Warrie was at the White House so much that the Johnsons began to think of her as their "third daughter," and Lady Bird felt that in this, as many other things, Warrie was a steadying influence on the sometimes impulsive Luci. But by the beginning of her father's new term in January of 1965, Luci had made a final decision; she wanted to be baptized into the Catholic Church on Friday, July 2, which would be her eighteenth birthday and would follow her June graduation from National Cathedral School.

The appointed day was fraught with mixed emotions. It was a celebratory day because of Luci's birthday, but it was also the tenth anniversary of the day Lyndon Johnson had suffered a major heart attack while serving as Senate majority leader, a health crisis that at one time seemed to shut the door on a run for the presidency. But Dwight Eisenhower had survived two heart attacks while he was president, and Johnson's recovery had been so complete that his physicians made it clear that there was no great risk of a recurrence. Still, the shadow of that crisis of ten years before hovered over the day of Luci's baptism. The ceremony at St. Matthew's Church in Washington was brief and private; word had not leaked to the press beforehand. Aside from the Johnson family, the presiding priest, Father Montgomery, and a few of Luci's Catholic friends who were sponsoring her, the only people in the church were a few elderly women praying privately. Warrie Lynn Smith was among the friends, of course, and so was a young man named Patrick Nugent, whom Luci would marry in a little more than a year. The ceremony would be followed by a festive birthday party in the Solarium of the White House.

Both Luci and Lynda had had a number of boyfriends over the years, some more serious than others. Lynda, in fact, had been engaged to a young military officer when her father became president, but that relationship had been broken off in April of 1964. The papers had carried a picture of Lynda and the young man captioned "The Last Dance," which Lady Bird had found both lovely and painful. It was another reminder to all of what a glass house the presidential mansion was — the press was always peering into it.

On Saturday, October 30, 1965, the media was overflowing with stories that Luci and Pat Nugent had shown up at the ranch, where the President was recovering from his gallbladder operation, and asked permission to marry. The news had supposedly been leaked by a "friend" in Austin. Lady Bird would note, "Pat's father was interviewed (he handled it very well). Pat's friends were interviewed," and the press "badgered and besieged" the White House press office until two in the morning. Lady Bird wondered, "If the government of Soviet Russia had fallen, would the news have received such concentrated attention?"

The press kept right on paying excessive attention to Luci and Pat even though the wedding wouldn't be taking place until the following August. Lady Bird wryly observed that although Luci was annoyed by the news coverage, she was praying for the members of the press. The media were not neglecting Lady Bird or Lynda, either. In late January 1966, Lady Bird wrote in her diary: "Two bits in the paper today. One was that the First Lady never would compete with the best dressed! Another was that 'the Beautiful People' are all heading for Acapulco and in the list of the beautiful people was Lynda Bird's name." One of the other people bound for Acapulco was the movie actor George Hamilton, whom Lynda was now seeing regularly.

The attention Lynda received in the daily newspapers because of her relationship with Hamilton was a good deal less colorful than what was written in the movie magazines and the new supermarket tabloid, the *National Enquirer*. This story reached a peak in April of 1966, when Hamilton took Lynda to the Academy Awards — at her very specific request, according to the gossip columns. *Inside Oscar*, the well-known book on Oscar history, notes that Lynda was so excited that she interrupted "a professor in a class at the University of Texas when he announced that he was giving a test the following Monday; 'I won't be here. I'm going to the Academy Awards that night with George Hamilton,' she shouted." She attended the ceremony wearing an orange dress with mink trim, upstaging a number of stars. Milton Berle, according to *Inside Oscar*, joked, "When I took out Woodrow Wilson's daughter, they didn't make such a fuss."

The Lynda and George story at times threatened to eclipse the upcoming marriage of Luci to Patrick Nugent — which was widely reported to have annoyed Luci.

Milton Berle's crack can't have helped — the last White House wedding had, in fact, been that of Woodrow Wilson's daughter Eleanor to the much older William G. McAdoo in 1917. That had been a simple ceremony. By contrast, Luci's wedding mass was to be celebrated at the Shrine of the Immaculate Conception, with a lavish reception to be held afterward at the White House. And that entailed vast preparations.

Lady Bird recalled that a number of funny things happened in making arrangements for the wedding, among them an amusing inscription:

The other day Bess and Simone gathered twenty-five startled tourists from the sightseers' line to stand them as props in a little roped-off enclosure in the East Room to enable them to measure the size of the area for the number of reporters who would cover the cake-cutting ceremony at the wedding. They were very obliging, although they had no idea why they were stand-ins.

The press wanted photographs of Luci in her wedding dress prior to the ceremony, but she didn't want Patrick Nugent to get even a glimpse of it before the wedding. *In-*

side the *White House* author Betty Boyd Caroli writes:

> *Great effort went into helping her keep the
> secret. J. B. West, chief usher, noted that the
> white gown was locked in the Lincoln Bed-
> room, and no one was permitted to enter.
> When Luci decided she wanted to be photo-
> graphed in the dress in the East Room, the
> entire White House had to be declared off-
> limits until she accomplished her mission.
> For an hour and a half, no one, not even the
> housecleaners, walked through the White
> House corridors. Chief Usher West recalled
> that there was "tighter security than there
> had been during the Cuban Missile Crisis."*

The Johnsons, with Luci's complete
agreement, tried to discourage presents
from foreign heads of state, emphasizing
that this was a private occasion. To assist in
making this rule stick, it was agreed that the
entire Diplomatic Corps, which consisted
of 114 member nations, would contribute to
a single gift. This was given to Luci and Pat
at a party on Monday, August 1, five days
before the wedding, hosted by Ambassador
at Large Averell Harriman and his wife,
Marie (he would marry the controversial
Pamela Digby Churchill Hayward after Ma-

rie's death) at their Washington home. The gift was an Old Maryland engraved silver tea service; Luci brought out piece after piece of this beautiful set in front of the assembled diplomats from around the world, including all the Soviet bloc countries.

On the Saturday morning of the wedding, Lady Bird went to Luci's bedroom and found her daughter eating breakfast while the famed hairdresser Jean-Louis combed out her hair. In the afternoon, while Luci was still dressing, Lady Bird went downstairs to find Lynda "running around the East Hall singing, 'Get Me to the Church on Time.' " She may not have been thinking only about Luci's date at the altar, since George Hamilton was among the wedding guests. The night before, in fact, Lady Bird had asked that a 1960 movie she had never seen be shown in the White House theater: *Home from the Hill*, which was set in Texas and was George Hamilton's first starring role.

The wedding service lasted more than an hour. Lady Bird was very happy with the mass itself and delighted with the fact that President Johnson didn't once look at his watch — "to his eternal credit." House Majority Leader Hale Boggs, also a Catholic, read the epistle at Luci's special request.

Lynda nearly fainted during the mass, but she refused help from two priests, until one brought a chair that she did sit in. Luci carried a rosary that Pope John XXIII had given to Lynda when she visited Rome — it was Luci's something borrowed — and at the end of the mass Archbishop Patrick O'Boyle read a telegram of congratulations that had arrived from Pope Paul VI. By the end of the ceremony Lynda had recovered, and she was able to join the best man (she was maid of honor) as expected in leaving the church.

The receiving line at the White House got under way in the Blue Room shortly after 2:30 in the afternoon. Then the cake was cut in the East Room. Lady Bird described it as a "great glistening Taj Mahal — seven tiers decorated with swans, white roses, and lacy arches like cathedral windows between the tiers, the whole edifice topped with a bouquet of lilies of the valley." It was after 6 P.M. when Luci and Pat left on their honeymoon. Even Lady Bird, who thought she knew how they were leaving, in the end wasn't sure what exit they had taken to dodge the press.

Lynda had graduated from the University of Texas at Austin at the beginning of June 1966 and taken a job with *McCall's* magazine in New York. With both daughters gone

— at least for the time being — the White House was a less lively and less homey place for their parents, who now had to depend more on telephone calls to keep in touch — calls that helped to alleviate the tension of the endless crises, large and small, that beset the modern presidency. The family was always together for major holidays, of course, and Lyndon and Lady Bird were often in Texas, where Luci and Pat were living in Austin, and there were periodic visits to New York City on official business that also allowed a chance to see Lynda in her new surroundings.

The next major family event took place on Wednesday, June 21, 1967, when, with her mother on hand, Luci Nugent gave birth to a son in Austin. The boy was named Patrick Lyndon Nugent and was soon answering to the name Lyn. Six weeks later, while Lynda was staying at the White House, Lady Bird suddenly awoke in the early morning with the sense that someone else was in the room. It was Lynda, and her mother immediately had an intuition what it was about. She started to suggest that they go back to Lynda's room, but by now her father was also awake, and Lynda told them both that she had fallen in love and wanted to get married. Her choice for a husband was not

George Hamilton — Lady Bird soon discovered that all the pictures of him were gone from Lynda's room — or anyone else glamorous or well-known. His name was Charles Robb. He had been in the marines for six years and was a military aide. He also had a degree in business administration from the University of Wisconsin, and his father worked for American Airlines. Lynda got all of this out and much more at about 4:00 A.M.

Chuck Robb was due to be posted to Vietnam, which meant that plans for a wedding would have to begin at once. Saturday, December 9, 1967, was chosen as the date, and this time the ceremony itself would take place in the White House. It was a military wedding, with the groom in uniform and the Marine Band playing the march from *Lohengrin.* Lynda entered the East Room on her father's arm wearing a white sheath wedding dress. The bridesmaids were dressed in red velvet — a color choice that Lady Bird had questioned but ended up finding exactly right. The wedding cake was cut, as is traditional at military weddings, with Chuck Robb's ceremonial sword.

Both daughters might now be married, but both of their husbands were serving in Vietnam within two months — a fact that did nothing to calm the anger of those who protested against the war. Luci and Lynda were now living in the White House again and would be there during the momentous events of 1968. To Luci's delight and Lynda's regret, their father announced in a televised address to the nation on April 1, 1968, that he would not seek or accept the nomination of his party for another term. Four days later, Martin Luther King Jr. was assassinated in Memphis, Tennessee. This horror was to be succeeded in two months, on June 5th, by the assassination of Robert F. Kennedy following his victory in the California presidential primary. By the time of the riot-torn Democratic convention in Chicago, Luci's sense that it was time for her father to get out of politics had been fully confirmed. The President had not even put in an appearance at the convention that nominated the man he had chosen as vice president, Hubert H. Humphrey, but Luci was there. She called it "the longest wake I ever attended."

With Richard Nixon's victory over Humphrey in November, the Johnson White House might have been a very sad place in the family's last months there. But they managed to be remarkably cheerful. Not long after the November election, Lady Bird and her daughters hosted the largest-ever gathering of former White House occupants. Among the former White House kids who attended were Alice Roosevelt Longworth; Helen Taft Manning, who had come home from Bryn Mawr to act as White House hostess for her father, William Howard Taft, when her mother had a stroke; Franklin Roosevelt's sons Elliot and John; Eleanor Seagraves, FDR's granddaughter, who had lived in the White House for two years as a child; and even the elderly granddaughters of Ulysses S. Grant and Benjamin Harrison.

Lynda Johnson Robb and Luci Johnson Nugent were thus profoundly aware of the special company they belonged to when they took the limousine ride from the White House to Capitol Hill for the inauguration of Richard Nixon in January of 1969. Eight years earlier the Johnson and Nixon families had made this same limousine journey together. Then Tricia and Julie Nixon's father had been the outgoing vice president and Lyndon Johnson the incoming one. Now Johnson would be leaving the White House, and the country, in Nixon's hands. Their daughters talked among themselves before the inauguration, one set of White House kids giving tips to another about how to live in the President's House.

9

⁓

The Nixon Girls

In her biography of her mother, *Pat Nixon: The Untold Story*, Julie Nixon Eisenhower vividly recalls inauguration day, January 20, 1969. As they waited for the ceremonies to begin at the Capitol, the Johnson and Nixon girls, along with their mothers, were sequestered in a small sitting room. Julie recalls that Lynda and Luci cried openly. "Finally they retreated to a bathroom for a few moments of privacy. During their last year in the White House, with both their husbands on active duty in Vietnam, the sisters had drawn much closer. Luci had taken me aside at the coffee to offer heartfelt advice: Don't let all the attention drive a wedge between you and Tricia."

Julie Nixon had married Dwight Eisenhower's grandson, David, on December 22, 1968. They were only twenty years old but had renewed their old acquaintanceship when they entered Smith and Amherst Colleges respectively in Northampton, Massachusetts (where Calvin Coolidge had begun his political career as the town's mayor), in the fall of 1966. They had wanted to be married in the summer of 1968, but because of Richard Nixon's decision to run for president again, they'd had to delay the wedding. Not only would a wedding have been a logistical problem in the middle of a presidential primary campaign, but everyone in the Nixon and Eisenhower families realized that it would likely be treated by the press as a political ploy. So the decision had been made to wait until December, by which time Julie's father would quite possibly be president-elect. Furthermore, if the wedding were to take place before Nixon was inaugurated, it could be conducted in relative privacy. And if he lost or failed to gain the nomination, the wedding could serve to restore family spirits.

Of course, Nixon did win the election, and Julie and her new husband would now be living at the White House when they were not attending college, while Tricia would become a full-time White House resident. The Nixon family had come very close to occupying the White House in 1960, and because of that earlier political defeat, their emotions were particularly high on inauguration day. Julie writes of approaching their new home after watching the parade:

In the dark, a light rain falling, we left the inaugural reviewing platform on foot for the short walk to the White House. A planked pathway had been built to guard against snow or mud, but despite the wood beneath our feet, we could still feel the intense cold of the former swampland that is Washington. Then, suddenly, in front of us was the most breathtakingly beautiful sight: the White House softly illuminated by the lights of the television crews.

At the end of that long first day, after visits to the inaugural balls, the Nixon family took a 2:00 A.M. tour of the White House. It was led by Julie's husband, David, whose years of playing in the house as a child meant that, like all White House kids, he knew it better than any president. He laughed about the note proclaiming "I will return" that he had left under a third-floor rug eight years earlier. Then, Julie writes, "he showed us the tiny room next to the second-floor elevator that had been his grandfather's painting studio; the hidden door to the passageway linking the second floor with the third; and even took us to the storage rooms on the third floor where he recognized a few pieces of his grandmother's wicker furniture, which had been removed from the solarium."

But what had been a playground for David could seem more like a prison to adults. Julie describes how Tricia tried to walk up from the first floor to her second-floor room above the Grand Entrance Hall that first night, only to hear a voice behind her saying not to try to open the doors because they were kept locked. It was a Secret Service agent, doing his job but giving Tricia an immediate lesson in one of the difficulties of living in the White House.

But within a few months they had learned to cope with the peculiarities of White House life. Tricia had supplied the White House telephone operators with a specific list of people she was willing to talk to, since young men who were absolute strangers took to calling and asking for dates. The White House operators, Tricia and Julie discovered, had an almost sixth sense about dealing with phone calls, seeming to know where every family member was at any given time and whether it was proper to disturb them. Tricia, as a permanent resident, hosted some events on her own and substituted for Pat Nixon at others when her mother was away. In the summer of 1969, with Julie and David also home, there was an increase in pleasant family events. But that summer Julie also acted as a guide for tourists taking the White House tours, focusing particularly on people who were either deaf or blind. Mrs. Nixon saw to it that tours tailored to those with disabilities were greatly increased during the Nixon years. That same summer, Tricia began tutoring students from Washington public schools, who would be brought to the White House in groups of two.

By this time the anti-Vietnam demonstrations that had become prevalent during the end of the Johnson administration became even larger and more vociferous. There were times when living in the White House became an ordeal simply because of the window-rattling roar of protestors beyond the grounds of the mansion. By the spring of 1970 student strikes were taking place at hundreds of colleges and universities across the country. Smith and Amherst were among those affected, and Julie and David were unable to attend their own graduations because of security concerns. Camp David, which Dwight Eisenhower had named for his grandson, became a regular retreat for the Nixon family when it wasn't possible for them to make a more extended visit to Key

Biscayne, Florida, to visit Nixon friend — and eventual Watergate figure — Bebe Rebozo or to the even more distant "Western White House," the home the Nixons owned in San Clemente, California. On June 6, 1970, the anniversary of D-Day, the family gathered at Camp David to celebrate the graduations of Julie and David from college and of David's sister, Susan, from high school. It was also the anniversary of the West Point graduation of David's father, John Eisenhower, which twenty-six years before had coincided with the launching of the Normandy invasion by the American and Allied forces under the command of his father, General Dwight Eisenhower. The former president had died in 1969, but Mamie Eisenhower was present for the occasion, as were David and Susan's parents, home from Belgium, where John was now the United States ambassador. Bebe Rebozo and other family friends tried hard to make it a festive day, but everyone was quietly aware of why Julie and David were not in Northampton with their classmates. Simply because they were the daughter and son-in-law of the President, they had become the object of obscene chants by some of the war protestors whom they had once gone to class with.

A gathering shaded by even more somber memories took place at the White House in January of 1971. Portraits of all United States presidents and first ladies hang in the White House, but they're moved from place to place according to the wishes of each successive occupant, who may want to display more prominently the predecessors of his — and no doubt one day her — own party or to give a particular place of honor to a former president or first lady who held special significance to the current occupants of the President's House.

President Kennedy's widow, now Jacqueline Onassis, had waited several years before commissioning portraits of herself and her assassinated husband. Now they were to be unveiled. Quite properly putting aside any personal feelings that might remain about the fact that John F. Kennedy had defeated her husband in 1960, Pat Nixon personally wrote to Mrs. Onassis, asking what her wishes were concerning the ceremony. Jacqueline Onassis didn't want to be part of a public ceremony with its press involvement, to shelter her own feelings and also those of her children, Caroline, then thirteen, and John, ten, whom she wanted to have see the portraits.

Thus arrangements were made for a private visit, which was kept secret not only from the White House press offices but from anyone on the White House staff who wouldn't be directly involved. Julie, Tricia, and their mother met Jackie and her children when they arrived and took them first to see the portrait of Jackie herself. "Although the children liked the portrait," Julie would later write, "they were both discerning: both commented on the hand, noting that their mother's did not resemble the unnaturally elongated, slender fingers the artist had painted." They then went to see the portrait of JFK in the Grand Entrance Hall. The children said they liked it, and Jackie thanked Pat Nixon "for displaying it so prominently." Tricia and Julie, with the three Nixon dogs, Pasha, Vicky, and King Timahoe, then traipsed up to the Solarium to look out over the lights of Washington at night. The two families had dinner together, and then the President showed John and Caroline the Oval Office and took them up to the Lincoln Bedroom so that they could sit on Lincoln's bed and make a wish according to time-honored tradition.

The Kennedy children wrote lively, appreciative thank-you notes, and Mrs. Onassis, in a separate letter to Pat Nixon, said, "The day I always dreaded turned out to be one of the most precious ones I have spent with my children." Once again, as in so many other times in American history, the White House had cast its unique spell. The families that have lived in the President's House always seem to ultimately find that that very special experience tends in the long run to override any ancient political enmity. To have lived in the White House makes one part of a clan that many aspire to join but that very few are privileged to enter into, and the members of that clan can understand one another in ways that might well have been impossible if they had not all lived in the White House.

The year 1971 would also bring another of those special events that unite modern presidents with those of the distant past: a White House wedding, the ninth in American history. Both Luci and Lynda Johnson had, of course, been married during their father's residency in the White House, in the television age, and the staff was well aware of the vast logistical problems such an event presents. But there are few happier occasions in the White House, and the dedicated professionals who run the mansion were delighted to undertake the job. Tricia Nixon, now twenty-five, had first met her husband-to-be, Edward Cox, at her senior-year dance at the Chapin School in New York City, which she and Julie had both attended when their father was practicing law in New York in the years between his defeat for the California governorship in 1962 and his second attempt at the presidency in 1968. Tricia had gone on from Chapin to New York's Finch College, while Ed Cox had attended Princeton University. Ed was now in his third year at Harvard Law School and would graduate just before the June 12, 1971, wedding date.

Julie's husband, David Eisenhower, was now in the navy, serving on the guided-missile cruiser USS *Albany*. He could not be at the wedding, but Julie would fly to see him in Athens, Greece, two days later, when his ship was due to put into port briefly. But David's grandmother Mamie was very much present at the wedding, and she was the first to go through the receiving line. The wedding day presented a quandary. The intention was to have the ceremony in the Rose Garden, but it drizzled all day long. Until the very last moment it looked as though the 4:00 ceremony would have to be moved indoors. "Finally, at four-fifteen," Julie later recalled, "my father received an Air Force weather report, which predicted that at four-thirty there would be a fifteen-minute clearing in the Washington area." He signaled the ushers to start seating the guests as quickly as possible, thus blithely canceling the painstaking, protocol-conscious seating plans. President Nixon began escorting Tricia from the Blue Room out to the South Portico and down the stairs and path leading to the Rose Garden. Tricia Nixon's elegant wedding gown, designed by Patricia Kidder, who was also a family friend and had created Julie's wedding dress in 1968, was much applauded by the press and the public; it was beautiful without being ostentatious. After the reception, Tricia was still dressed in her gown as she and Ed left by the North Portico for their honeymoon, accompanied by the traditional shower of rice.

Tricia would not live permanently in the White House again, although she and Ed often came down from their New York apartment to visit. Julie was usually there, but she sometimes flew off to visit David when his ship was in a foreign port. The White House sometimes felt like a beleaguered fortress as the Vietnam War dragged on, and the protests against it continued on a regular basis with occasional outbursts of fury. The 1972 presidential campaign —

which pitted Richard Nixon against Democratic Senator George McGovern of South Dakota, a long-time critic of the war — was a strident one that saw the country as sharply divided as it had been in a long time. But even some of those who were disturbed by the continuing war were swayed by Republican charges that McGovern was a left-wing radical tied to the forces of "acid, abortion, and amnesty." The reference to acid was prompted by the use of the drug LSD by hippies, almost all of them left wing in their politics, the abortion reference concerned the *Roe v. Wade* case, which was initially argued before the Supreme Court in 1972, although not decided until the following year; and the amnesty issue was a reminder of the debate about what to do in respect to the thousands of young American men who had fled to Canada or other countries to avoid service in Vietnam. In the end, Nixon's victory in November 1972 was of landslide proportions, as he won by more than 17 million votes over McGovern and carried every state except Massachusetts and the District of Columbia.

January 1973 brought the death of former President Lyndon Johnson on the twenty-second, Nixon's second inauguration on the twenty-fourth, and the signing of a long-delayed peace treaty with North Vietnam on the twenty-seventh. But all would be eventually overwhelmed by the formal start of investigations by the Congress, still controlled by the Democrats, into what would come to be known as Watergate. The vote to proceed with investigations had been taken on January 11, and in the months to come the events triggered by what was called a "third-rate burglary" of the Democratic headquarters at the Watergate complex the previous year would cause the Nixon administration to unravel and lead to explosive impeachment hearings in Congress.

President Nixon's wife and daughters rarely had involved themselves with political decisions — Nixon did not want them involved for their own sakes — but Watergate inevitably caught them up in its web as well. In late April, just after David Eisenhower had been released from the navy and was staying with his wife at the White House, Tricia came down from New York for a weekend visit. The President was at Camp David; his two daughters and son-in-law waited until Pat Nixon had gone to bed at the White House, then discussed which of them should tell the President that he must demand the resignations of his two most important aides, Bob Haldeman and John Erlichman, who were being identified in the press as having been deeply involved with the Watergate break-in. Tricia went up to Camp David Saturday morning to convey their consensus, which apparently steeled her father to take action before the day was over.

But nothing could stanch the wounds of Watergate. Matters seemed to get worse every day, with each revelation taking the case closer to the Oval Office itself. Once the existence of the White House tapes was revealed, the Nixon presidency started unraveling at a devastating pace. During this period, Julie and Tricia's main job was to try to bolster their mother, who was herself trying to lift the spirits of her distracted and gloomy husband. As the end approached, in late June of 1974, Pat Nixon, Tricia, and Julie all wanted the President to fight on. It was Julie whom he first confided to that he was going to resign, during a brief conversation in his second office in the Executive Office Building across from the White House. Julie went back across to the mansion and called her husband at his law school in Washington and then her sister in New York, who said she would immediately fly down. Then Julie went to tell her mother.

"Her mouth began to tremble," Julie would later write of her mother. "We embraced for a moment, our arms around each other very lightly, barely touching, knowing that if we drew any closer we would both break down and not let go. When I stood back I saw that Mother had tears in her eyes. For me, those tears that were shed so briefly were perhaps the saddest moment of the last days in the White House."

The last ordeal was the farewell to the White House staff and the cabinet on the morning of August 9, 1974, before departing for San Clemente and another, very different, life. The farewell was to be televised, much to Pat Nixon's distress. Just before going to the East Room, Tricia told her mother and sister a friend's advice about controlling the urge to sob, instructing them to take three deep breaths. They did, and then Pat, Julie and David, and Tricia and Ed went to listen to Richard Nixon speak one last time in the White House.

The years ahead would sometimes be difficult for the Nixons and their daughters. But they had their moments of joy, as well. Tricia and Ed had a son, Christopher, and have always kept a low profile. Julie and David had three children, and both have had best-selling books, Julie with her biography of her mother and David with one of his grandfather. Richard Nixon went on to write many books and be sought out for advice on foreign affairs — on which he was considered one of the savviest of presidents — by all his successors in the White House. After several strokes, Pat Nixon died in 1995, and the former president followed her in 1996. His memorial service was attended by President Clinton, former Presidents Ford, Carter, and Bush and their wives as well as former First Ladies Lady Bird Johnson and Nancy Reagan. While Richard Nixon may have departed Washington in disgrace, the unique clan of White House occupants gathered as they always do to say farewell to one of their own and warmly console the grieving daughters who had once called the White House their home.

10

∾

Fun-Loving Fords

No president ever found himself occupying the White House under such peculiar and roundabout circumstances as Gerald Ford. Under the Twenty-fifth Amendment to the Constitution — which became law in 1967 — Ford had been named by President Nixon to replace Vice President Spiro Agnew, who resigned as part of a plea bargain concerning charges of bribe-taking while governor of Maryland. After being approved by both houses of Congress, as the law required, in December of 1973, Ford then succeeded to the presidency itself following President Nixon's resignation on August 9, 1974. The Nixons were already in flight to California before Ford's swearing-in ceremony, and he thus became not only the first unelected president but also the first to move instantly into the White House. In all previous unexpected successions, the vice president had had to wait while the widow and children of a deceased president made arrangements to leave.

The new first family consisted of President Ford, First Lady Betty Ford, three sons — Mike, born March 14, 1950; Jack, born March 16, 1952; and Steve, born May 19, 1956 — and one daughter — Susan, born July 16, 1957. Only Susan was a full-time resident of the White House. Mike was studying to become a minister in Massachusetts, Jack was at Utah State University, and Steve would soon flee Washington to work on a ranch in Montana.

Steve decided very quickly that life in the White House wasn't for him. He made an expensive mistake almost immediately, having a late-night party for twenty-five of his friends on the third floor of the White House while his parents were sound asleep in the second-floor family quarters. A week later President Ford summoned his son to the Oval Office and waved a bill in front of him. It was for the refreshments he had ordered up from the White House kitchen for his pals. Steve had assumed that they were paid for by the government as part of the White House expenses. No such luck. Steve had to repay his father for the supposedly secret party.

Many people don't realize that the first family pays for its own food while residing in the White House. Official functions, whether a tea for congressional wives or a state dinner, are indeed paid for by the U.S. government. But if a dozen relatives show up for the Christmas holidays, every bite they eat comes out of the pockets of the president and first lady. The president's salary is peanuts compared with what top corporate executives make, and many presidents and their wives have been aghast at the cost of living in the White House.

But quite aside from this early encounter with the financial rules of his new abode, Steven Ford wasn't happy with the media attention and the general hubbub of the White House. Like all White House kids, though, he was fascinated by the secret passages and stairways that abound in the mansion, and he found the staff to be very friendly. Looking back in 1992, in an interview with the *Cleveland Plain Dealer*, he recalled that the first friend he made was the White House chef, when he wandered into the kitchen looking for potato chips. But he felt stultified by the general atmosphere. "At eighteen years old, it was not my style. You just felt like you were living in a museum. That was a little tough. You had to make this place your home. I always tried to be myself, not let the place intimidate me." But within three weeks he had decided that the prospect of either living in the White House or moving into a freshman college dorm with ten Secret Service agents following him around was too much to deal with. So he persuaded his parents to let him spend the next two years working on a cattle ranch in Montana. Even there, though, he couldn't escape the entourage of Secret Service agents.

The agents would come to Montana on two-week rotations, and Steve found it fun to introduce them to ranch life — something he had been familiar with for years. "It was like — what was that Billy Crystal movie? — *City Slickers*, fifteen years before they ever did the movie," Ford told the *Plain Dealer*. Once, when he and a ranch hand were sent out in search of lost cattle in foul, wet weather, the Secret Service agent sent with him decided on the second day to stay by the truck while Steve and the other hand went off on horseback. After all, how many kidnappers would be out in such a remote area with the rain pelting down? But Steve had an idea for a little fun as they returned. After firing off a rifle a few times, he "slung himself over his saddle as if he were dead."

"This Secret Service guy, you can imagine," Steve recounted. "The first printable words out of his mouth were, 'My career, my career.' " But despite such pranks he would become good friends with many of the agents, and he is still in touch with them. In the early 1980s, Steve Ford was even the host of an NBC series called *Secret Service*, which he was proud of doing because it gave him a chance to celebrate the agents who had twice saved his father's life while he was president.

Although all three Ford sons came home often enough to cause their mother to note that a "lot of courting" went on in the third-floor Solarium, which had always been a retreat for presidential kids, it was Susan Ford, known as Suze to her family and friends, who as a permanent White House resident got most of the press coverage. Just seventeen when she moved into the White House, Susan was already attending the Holton Arms School in Bethesda, Maryland. She has said that one advantage of having been raised and schooled in Washington while her father served in Congress was that a move into the White House didn't mean she had to change schools or leave friends behind, as is usually the case for the children of presidents. As reported by Betty Ford in her memoir, *The Times of*

My Life, Susan was given advice by Alice Roosevelt Longworth, then in her ninetieth year, about living in the White House: "Have a helluva good time," she wrote to Susan — and her mother said that the advice was taken.

"Having a good time," Mrs. Ford noted, "involved Susan's realizing that she couldn't make everyone in the United States happy, and she might as well stop worrying about it." Betty Ford quotes her daughter on the criticism she got during the White House years: " 'I was criticized for everything from wearing blue jeans to dating Brian [McCartney, a Vail, Colorado, ski patrol member], who was nine years older than I, to being given a muskrat coat . . . because muskrats are trapped, not bred.' "

The family had long been going to Vail for ski vacations, and Susan had made many friends there, but her mother was somewhat perturbed when her daughter, at eighteen, said that she and Brian wanted to get married. Betty Ford didn't dislike Brian, but he was indeed nine years older than her daughter; Betty didn't think Susan was ready for marriage and wouldn't be happy for long in the rather insular community of Vail, a great place to visit but . . . Mrs. Ford was well aware that her forceful opposition was only likely to increase the intensity of the romance, and so she decided to let things run their course. When Brian and two of his friends came to stay at the White House for Susan's eighteenth birthday party, however, Betty made clear to them all that there was to be "no trespassing" in one another's third-floor bedrooms, and any socializing was to be done in the Solarium.

Despite this restriction, Susan remembers her eighteenth birthday bash as the high point of her White House years. It was celebrated a day early, on the fifth of July, because that was a Saturday and it also meant that out-of-town guests could watch the Fourth of July fireworks from the Truman Balcony of the White House.

There was a dance floor laid out on the South Lawn, under a clump of trees, and picnic tables all around, and we had hamburgers and hot dogs on a grill, and beer in plastic cups. Heinz Bender [the White House pastry chef] had made me a birthday cake in the shape of a camera — a tribute to my hoped-for career — and a rock band, friends of mine from Vail, played a song with lyrics dedicated to me.

Later the group headed down to a

Georgetown bar called Winston's, where it was a house tradition to throw a pie in the face of anyone celebrating their birthday, and Susan obviously enjoyed this ritual. She stayed out all night, in fact. Presidents don't have to wait up for celebrating daughters, of course, since these daughters are accompanied by the Secret Service. Susan admitted to having a dreadful hangover the next day, and her mother noted that it would be two years, until her twentieth birthday, celebrated in Vail, that Susan stayed out that late again.

While her White House birthday party was deemed a great success, Susan apparently had mixed feelings about her school's senior prom, which had also been held at the White House several weeks earlier. She has sometimes mentioned this as another cherished memory, but in her mother's book she is quoted as saying, "We couldn't serve beer because we'd have had to get a slip from each student's parents saying they approved, which would have been a pain in the neck. . . . Our headmaster was a pain in the neck, too."

That summer Susan worked as a photographer on a newspaper in Topeka, Kansas, then entered the Washington, D.C., women's college Mount Vernon in the fall.

By her own admission her curriculum included a major in partying. And Susan was not the only party animal among the Ford children. Jack was famous for it, and tales of his exploits sometimes got into the press. But he kept himself out of any real trouble, and the worst the press could come up with was a published rumor that he had spent the night with a girlfriend in the Lincoln Bedroom. Since Jack was a son rather than a daughter — and older by several years — it may be that his mother hadn't given him her "no trespassing" lecture.

Oddly, the biggest public outcry about the Ford children developed out of an interview Betty Ford gave to Morley Safer on *60 Minutes*. He surprised her by asking what she would do if Susan came home and told her she was having an affair. The First Lady replied, "Well, I wouldn't be surprised. I think she's a perfectly normal human being, like all young girls. If she wanted to continue it, I would certainly counsel and advise her on the subject. And I'd want to know pretty much all I could about the young man." In her memoir, Mrs. Ford adds, "What I'd been trying to say was that while I couldn't condone an affair, I wouldn't kick my daughter out of the house for having one."

Public reaction to the interview was intense. Many people, among them Bing Crosby, said that they would kick their daughters out. In her memoirs, Betty Ford was good sport enough to report on what Jimmy Carter, who would subsequently defeat her husband for the presidency, replied when he was asked how he would feel if his daughter told him she was having an affair: "Carter said he'd be 'shocked and overwhelmed,' and added, 'My daughter is seven years old.'" Mrs. Ford had also failed on the program, in the view of some, to take a sufficiently hard line against drugs, and she infuriated many right-wing Republicans by saying, not for the first time, that she supported the Supreme Court's *Roe v. Wade* decision legalizing abortion.

Susan would later admit to her mother that Betty's answer about the possibility of Susan having an affair bothered her — she was afraid it might suggest to boys that she was "easy." But at the time, Mrs. Ford recalls, "Susan told reporters she had no affair to confess, Mike told reporters he didn't agree with all of his mother's views, Jack told reporters he'd smoked marijuana but never used hard drugs, and Steve told reporters nothing."

Fishbowl though the White House is, reporters don't get wind of every embarrassing moment. One of Betty Ford's favorites concerned Jack, who was home at the White House when a state dinner was given for Queen Elizabeth II. He had to rent a tuxedo and then couldn't find the shirt studs for it. As his mother remembers, "Jerry and I were bringing the royal couple upstairs in the elevator when it stopped on the second floor, the doors opened, and Jack came flying in, still fiddling with his shirt front. He stood there, mouth open, gaping at the four of us, and the Queen of England turned to me and smiled sweetly. 'I have one just like it at home,' she said."

At least Jack hadn't been running naked down the corridor like Caroline Kennedy.

11

⁓

The Carter Clan

The story made headlines all across the country: Amy Carter was going to be enrolled in public school while her father served as president of the United States.

The last White House kid to go to public school in Washington had been Theodore Roosevelt's son Archie, in 1906. And he hadn't needed to be accompanied by Secret Service agents in those quieter, simpler times. Sending Amy, who was nine years old when the Carters took up residence in the White House in January of 1977, to public school was very much in keeping with her father's political image and philosophy. While Jimmy Carter was probably the most intellectual president since Woodrow Wilson, he had emphasized his homespun side in his run for the White House, and even as president he started out by carrying his own garment bag onto *Air Force One* to symbolize his lack of pretension.

Still, there was considerable controversy about Jimmy and Rosalynn Carter's decision concerning their daughter's education. Some critics said that they were sacrificing Amy's best interests to political imagery, while others suggested that it was unfair to the ordinary kids who would be her classmates to subject them to the intrusive presence of the Secret Service. The fact that both of Amy's parents were great champions of the public school system in America and had attended public schools themselves was seen by many as beside the point.

In fact, the majority of the voters cheered the decision — but it was an indication of how much Amy's life was about to change that polls were actually taken on the subject. And Amy and her parents may well have had second thoughts on her first day of school. Rosalynn Carter would later write in her autobiography, *First Lady from Plains*, "We stepped from the car into a barrage of news reporters, television and flash cameras, and spectators who crowded around her as she trudged with her books toward the door. We made it through, Amy having already learned to look straight ahead, smile, and keep walking. But this morning, she wasn't smiling."

Within a couple of weeks the other children at the school had gotten used to having a president's daughter and her guards in their midst, and Amy had little trouble making friends. In the months to follow, she sometimes brought other girls from the school home to the White House for overnights, and they were allowed to share the big bed in the Lincoln Bedroom, "and stay awake half the night listening for Lincoln's ghost," as Rosalynn fondly recalls. A tree house was built for Amy on the South Lawn, and in the summer she and her friends would sometimes sleep there — meaning that long-suffering Secret Service agents would have to be posted on the grounds below.

Amy had three older brothers, John Williams, called Jack, born in 1947; James Earl III, always called Chip; and Donnel Jeffrey, known as Jeff. Chip, born in 1950, and Jeff, two years younger, both lived in the White House with their wives, but Jack and his wife and son remained in Calhoun, Georgia, where he was in partnership with his father-in-law as an attorney. Jeff transferred from Georgia State in Atlanta to Washington's George Washington University, while Chip went to work for the Democratic National Committee. Chip, who had already served on his hometown city council in Plains, Georgia, had campaigned for eighteen months with his father and was the most politically oriented of all the children.

When the Carters took up residence in the White House, Amy was given the noisy bedroom over the central hall where tourists entered the house, which previously had been occupied by Caroline Kennedy, Luci Johnson, and Tricia Nixon. The desk she did her homework on in that room had been used for letter writing by First Lady Eleanor Roosevelt. To a greater extent than most presidential families, the thrifty Carters explored the warehouse where the furnishings of former White House occupants were stored. There was, Rosalynn Carter would later report, "an adorable little sofa and chair set for Amy, which had been given to Caroline Kennedy while her father was president" but was never used. Chip and his wife, Caron, chose a chiffonier from the Truman White House plus a small toy chest for their new baby daughter, Sarah. Unlike Amy's furniture, the chest had actually been used by Caroline Kennedy. "Jeff and Annette chose the greatest treasure of all: a chair Mary Todd Lincoln had purchased."

In later years Chip was the only one of the Carter children willing to talk much about living in the White House, in spite of the fact that he and his first wife, Caron, had divorced during President Carter's term. He told a reporter from the *Atlanta Journal and Constitution* in 1992 that the fishbowl aspects of the White House adversely affected the marriage. "I think that once we started having problems, it became other people's business so much that there was no possibility of us ever working anything out," he said, but adding that he took "full responsibility" for the breakup of the marriage.

After Caron left him, Chip continued to live at the White House, leading to spurious press stories about his new "bachelor" status. "I was accused of putting a nude woman in the dumbwaiter of the White House and sending her from the third floor down to the kitchen and it getting broken halfway down at three o'clock in the morning." The press had elaborated by saying that workmen had had to break through a wall on the second floor to release the naked beauty. "It never happened," Chip said. "But it was written as fact, and I'm sure that everybody just assumed it happened." This story suggests that even though there has been plenty of hanky-panky in the White House over the last two hundred years, some of it is completely fictional.

"Amy was young," Chip Carter told the interviewer in 1992, "and she probably handled it better than the rest of us, but it also made her an extremely private person, which is the reason she's not doing this interview and I am." Back in Plains, Amy had run a lemonade and sandwich stand in her front yard — hardly something she could do at the White House. But there were plenty of new activities to keep her busy. Some of those, like roller skating through the grand East Room, were regarded by critics as a little too boisterous. But Amy also got to participate in more decorous ventures. A new tour guide to the White House was published, in which several of the Carters had had a hand. As reported by the *Washington Post*, the thirteen-page color guide, simply titled *The White House*, had a foreword written by Jimmy Carter, while "his son Jeff and daughter-in-law Annette took the photographs, Amy Carter conducts the pictorial 'tour,' and the wives of two presidential aides wrote the text." The *Post* noted, "Among the booklet's 17 color photographs is one of President Carter holding his 10-year-old daughter, Amy, in his lap at his desk in the Oval Office. Another shows Amy, wearing a long white dress, standing in the White House Entrance Hall."

Amy once got to perform for White House guests, like such predecessors as Margaret Wilson and Margaret Truman, though on a smaller scale. After a luncheon for King Baudouin and Queen Fabiola of Belgium, there was entertainment by the New York Harp Ensemble and then a short performance of a children's Suzuki violin group, which included Amy. Six young musicians, one only seven and far more advanced than Amy, not only charmed the king and queen with their talent but took on the Marine String Band, as well. On their way out, as the children passed the Marine Band, which was playing a Beethoven piece, "they stopped, tucked violins under chins, and joined in without missing a note," Amy's proud mother would later write.

But Amy got an unfavorable reaction when the press reported that she had been allowed to attend a state dinner, during which she pulled out a book and began reading. The media treated this as some kind of scandal, obviously unaware that Amy was merely following precedent: At the age of twelve, Charlie Taft had taken along a copy of *Treasure Island* to read during his father's 1909 inauguration. The press uproar over Amy's supposed gaffe infuriated Lillian Carter, her outspoken grandmother, who announced that the Carter family had always read at meals. That, she added, seemed a much better way to spend one's time at the dinner table than arguing, the way most people did.

As often happens to White House kids, Amy got no press coverage at all on the many occasions when she behaved extremely well in a difficult situation. One time, for example, the White House held a reception to promote an energy conservation program especially designed to encourage the participation of young people. The reception was attended by several hundred children, who were to be entertained by the Campbell Soup Kids and Marvel Comics stars like Spider-Woman and the Incredible Hulk. As a White House kid, Amy's participation was important, and she'd been looking forward to it. But that morning she'd had her braces tightened — perhaps a little too much, since she was in tears from the pain. Her mother suggested that she go upstairs and lie down for a while, but Amy went out and joined the party instead.

Through no fault of her own, Amy later

figured in a headline-making event that adversely affected her father's reelection campaign. Debating Republican presidential candidate Ronald Reagan on television, President Carter quoted Amy on the subject of nuclear disarmament — Amy had participated in long discussions about that subject at school, and her father had talked about it with her, too. But the press and the voters were aghast that a teenager should be quoted on such a serious subject, even if her father was president. The cartoonists pounced on the issue, and some Republicans suggested that Amy was really running the country. In fact, when the president had used Amy's quote during a debate rehearsal, aides advised him to drop it, but he refused, and there was no question that it hurt him at the polls. Even Rosalynn Carter would later say it was a bad mistake.

After losing the election, the Carters returned to their peanut farm in Plains, Georgia. In 1984, when Amy began attending a boarding school in Atlanta, Rosalynn Carter looked back at the difficult first months after leaving the White House. She said that Amy had loved Washington and missed the friends she had made there a great deal. "She told me once, 'You may be a country girl, but I'm not. I grew up in the city.' " She had been only three when her father became governor of Georgia, and the family had moved to Atlanta. And then there had been the four years in Washington, going to a public school, as she had in Atlanta, with city kids. "When we came home," Rosalynn Carter said, "I found that she did not want to make new friends because she missed the ones she had made in Washington so much. She feared she would forget them if she made new friends."

Such fears affect many children whose parents move often because of their jobs. Steve Ford has said that when his family moved into the White House, his father warned them right at the start to remember that it was only temporary housing. It proved for both his father and for his successor, Jimmy Carter, to be more temporary than either of them would have liked. That was fine by Steve, a young man with his own agenda by the time his father became president. He hadn't liked the White House, anyway. But for Amy, as for many young children of presidents before her, leaving the White House was a real blow. To younger White House kids it can become home in a way that their older counterparts have a difficult time understanding.

12

∾

Reagans Make Headlines

Although at seventy Ronald Reagan was the oldest man ever to be sworn in to a first term as president, when he was inaugurated in January of 1981, he still had two children under thirty. He also had two older children — daughter Maureen, born in 1941, and an adopted son, Michael, born in 1946 — from his first marriage to actress Jane Wyman, who won the Oscar for Best Actress in *Johnny Belinda* in 1948, when the marriage was already under stress. She had been the bigger star almost from the start and didn't like the amount of time he spent working as president of the Screen Actors Guild, beginning in 1947. They were divorced in 1949.

Ronald Reagan then married a younger actress, Nancy Davis, on March 4, 1952. Their first child, Patti, was born on October 22, 1952 — a birth date that caused Nancy

Reagan to comment in her memoir of the White House years, *My Turn,* "Go ahead and count." Ron Jr. was born nearly six years later, on May 20, 1958, and was only twenty-three when his father became president. This "blended family," as Nancy Reagan termed it, would create more news stories about family squabbles than perhaps any other first family in White House history.

In her memoir, Nancy Reagan is remarkably frank about these problems, while understandably suggesting that they were occasionally blown out of proportion by the press. But she is also sometimes defensive to the point of bitterness about the fact that the public seemed to blame her for the difficulties she had with her children. The public, of course, was basing its view on the highly publicized criticisms that flowed from her children at various points.

The fact that the children spent little time at the White House — except when Maureen lived there for a while during her father's second term — did nothing to curtail press coverage of the family's many disagreements and may well have contributed to the problem. All of the kids complained at one time or another of feeling that they were being ignored. Ron Jr., who complained the least, nevertheless would pin-point the kinds of problems that arose in an interview he gave to *Newsday* after his father left office. He noted, for example, that no one told him that his parents had sold the house he had grown up in. "I knew it was on the market. But I was quietly pissed that somebody hadn't bothered to pick up the phone and say, 'By the way . . .' " He was also utterly surprised at the news that Nancy Reagan had been consulting an as-trologer, Joan Quigley, thinking at first that it was just a "media joke." But then he saw Sam Donaldson talking about it with com-plete seriousness on *This Week with David Brinkley.* "So I finally called up and found out it was real, which was just as big a sur-prise to me as anyone else."

But Ron generally kept his problems to himself while his father was president, un-like Maureen and, especially, Michael and Patti. Michael was the first of the Reagan children to end up in the doghouse after his father was elected. As the *Washington Post* reported:

Michael, 39, is the adopted son of Reagan and his first wife, Jane Wyman. His rela-tions with Nancy Reagan, always cool, chilled to the freezing point in 1981 when

Michael wrote letters to several air bases on behalf of a Burbank-based airplane parts company, Dana Ingalls Profile Inc., that he was vice president of at the time. "I know that with my father's leadership at the White House, this country's armed services are going to be rebuilt and strengthened," the letter said. "We at Dana Ingalls Profile want to be involved in that process."

Nancy Reagan apparently thought that this was trading far too openly on a familial relationship, and she said publicly that Michael had "made a mistake." There was a considerable uproar in the press, and Michael resigned from the company. He and his family were conspicuously absent from Reagan family occasions, and in an interview with columnist Betty Beale at Thanksgiving in 1984, Nancy Reagan said, "There is an estrangement from Michael, and there has been for three years." Michael and his wife, Colleen, had two children, Ashley Marie and Cameron. They were the President's only grandchildren, and Michael used this fact to strike back hard at his stepmother after her Thanksgiving interview, saying that Nancy was "jealous" because she was not really their grandmother. He pointed out that the Reagans had never even met twenty-one-month-old Ashley.

By December of 1984, the press was paying a great deal of attention to this "Reagan Family Feud," as it was routinely called, and a major attempt was made by the President to patch things up. Ronald Reagan called his son Michael, "but," *Newsweek* detailed, "Michael hung up on him, according to the White House, which also reported that Reagan subsequently called Michael daily from Washington to try smoothing over family differences. The President failed to persuade his son to drop his television appearance, though Michael did moderate his complaints on the air."

The uproar was finally contained just after Christmas 1984, when the Reagans were in California and met with Michael in a "plush $3,000-a-night suite" at a Los Angeles hotel on December 27. Nancy and the President finally met Ashley, gifts were exchanged, and afterward Nancy issued a statement through the White House press office saying, "It was a nice visit. There are no differences. All is resolved." Lou Cannon of the *Washington Post* revealed that this message had been tacked to the bulletin board "in the White House press briefing room in the Century Plaza Hotel" the day after the meeting. Cannon added that one

White House official said to frustrated reporters, "I'm in the same boat you are. I wish this thing would get over with so we could all have a decent New Year's weekend."

It would not come out until later, in Nancy's memoir and Michael's own book, that when the President called Michael at Thanksgiving, his son had said, "I wish I had never been adopted by you." In his book, *On the Outside Looking In*, Michael revealed that he was one of those adopted children who had always been troubled by the idea that he had not been wanted by his birth mother. Those feelings had been intensified by the Reagan-Wyman divorce and his difficulty in feeling comfortable in the new blended family that developed when Nancy and his father had children of their own. He developed a defensive sense of humor that was sometimes offensive to the rest of the family, making cracks about all of them at various points during the Reagan presidency, and doing things like having a T-shirt made up that read I AM NOT THE DANCER — as though anyone would mistake the stocky Michael for his lithe younger brother, Ron. He would ultimately recognize that he was striking out at the rest of the family because he undervalued himself. He was trying to work through these problems while his father was president, and the fact that Reagan *was* president didn't make things any easier. Eventually Michael would come to a much greater degree of mutual understanding with his family, but the process caused heartache all around and led to many news stories during the White House years.

Michael's older sister, Maureen, had her own differences with her parents at various times, but they certainly didn't stem from any lack of confidence. As the older child of Reagan and Wyman and their biological child, as well, she was less deeply affected by the divorce, although she found the new circumstances quite strange at times. Visiting Nancy and her father when Patti was a little girl — and meeting her half sister for the first time — she found that Patti was excited to have just learned that she had a brother — Michael — who had also recently visited. Maureen asked Patti if she knew what that meant Maureen was. Patti didn't, and Maureen told her that they were sisters, which caused Patti to run crying from the room. Ronald Reagan told Maureen that they just hadn't gotten around to explaining the whole story yet to Patti.

Over the years the relationship between

Maureen and Nancy was, both have admitted, somewhat on-again, off-again, but Maureen was too independent and self-sufficient to let it get her down. As the most political of the children — she liked to say she had been a Republican longer than her father, who had not fully switched parties until the 1960 Kennedy-Nixon race — Maureen had campaigned diligently for her father, although she disagreed with him on abortion and women's rights issues. During her father's first term, however, she had been angered by the fact that her father didn't openly support her when she ran for the Republican nomination to the U.S. Senate from California in 1982. Both her father and Nancy thought she should have started out by running for a lesser office — and the public seemed to agree, nominating Pete Wilson, who won the seat and later became the two-term governor of California.

In the end, Maureen proved an invaluable asset to her father as an emissary to women voters because of her more liberal positions on women's issues. And during Reagan's second term he rewarded her by seeing to it that she was chosen as co-chair of the Republican Party, which for many years had had male and female co-chairs. Thus during her father's second term she was often in

Washington, and she always stayed at the White House, usually in the Lincoln Bedroom, which she loved. During this period, she and Nancy established a warmer rapport than ever before, and even though she was the oldest Reagan child, she ended up being far more of a "White House kid" than any of her siblings. In fact, she found herself in the odd position of being much closer to her stepmother than Nancy and Ronald Reagan's own daughter, Patti Davis, who had taken her mother's maiden name when Ronald Reagan became governor of California. In her memoir, Nancy Reagan writes that her relationship with Patti "has been one of the most painful and disappointing aspects of my life. . . . Somehow, no matter what I do, we seem to square off. And it's been this way from the start." During the White House years, there was even more trouble between Nancy and Patti than there was with Michael. The nadir came with the publication of Patti's 1986 book *Home Front*, coauthored with writer Maureen Strange, which her mother describes as "a thinly disguised, self-pitying autobiographical novel about a young woman with left-wing politics whose conservative father becomes president." The novel was particularly hard on the "clothes-horse" mother in the story.

Nancy Reagan was not only hurt but surprised by the book, since Patti had started writing it not long after her 1984 wedding to yoga instructor Paul Grilley, an occasion she had sought out her mother's help for and that had gone very well.

In interviews at the time of the book's publication in March of 1986, Patti was defensive about the issue of hurting her parents' feelings. "I've been reading all this stuff about my mother being so hurt about the book that she won't open it, which if you think that through doesn't make a lot of sense," she told the *Washington Post*. "What's so shocking — what book did everybody read? It's as though I wrote some nonfiction exposé and told everybody's secrets." Stressing that it was a novel, she added, "I wrote a mother. It could have been her, it could have been any number of women during the '60s and '70s." She added that she thought the mother in the novel was "a very sympathetic character, and very funny in the quirks she had developed, trying to identify with her children through using their language and consistently getting it wrong."

Patti told the *Post* that a particularly autobiographical moment in the novel came at the beginning, when the heroine, having just come from her father's inauguration as president, looks out from the White House and sees the tourists pressed up against the fences around the mansion. "She thinks that they look like outsiders and she feels like an outsider." Three years earlier, in an interview with *People,* Patti had said that she had "dreaded" her father being elected president. "I said that I couldn't handle that — and I didn't. Right after the inauguration I got really sick. I couldn't breathe and had to be taken to the hospital emergency ward. It was stress. My whole body went into shock."

But she bounced back. She had always been what *People* called a "free spirit . . . Last year, while her father was sounding the cry for a strong nuclear defense, Patti was busy appearing at antinuke rallies. She's lived with the Eagles' guitarist, Bernie Leadon, and has had a highly publicized fling with the actor Peter Strauss." At the time of the *People* interview in the summer of 1983, Patti was acting in summer stock as one of the three young women who made up the entire cast of the Off-Broadway hit *Vanities.* Her two costars, Susan Bigelow and Marsha Korb, had far more legitimate theater experience but found to their surprise that Patti was not only up to the job but also, ac-

191

cording to Ms. Korb, "a fascinating person — so open and caring." Patti's parents didn't get to see her performance, but Patti excused them on the grounds of a short run and the fact that "they are sensitive about upstaging either my brother Ronnie or me. If they came, it would become their show."

While Patti always said it was nonsense that her parents didn't even invite her to the White House, as some press reports had it, and that she was welcome any time, she didn't go to Washington often. In 1983 she maintained that she preferred to see her parents in the more relaxed atmosphere of their California ranch. But in 1986 she would also say that Washington was "not my world. It's a very overwhelming world. The White House and the presidency is big stuff. It's not really my interest."

In interviews Patti has always seemed to understand that she and her parents quite simply had different objectives and agendas. She told the *Washington Post* that reports about the Reagans being distant from their children were "valid only in the sense that I think anybody with as large an ambition as the presidency is remote because it's an all-consuming job . . . some of the energy has to be taken from other things." She also thought that the fact that all the Reagan kids were "out of the house and living our own lives" contributed to the public sense of distance between parents and children. But that had not seemed to be the case with the grown Carter sons, nor would it be so with the grown Bush children. While Patti often gave the impression that she understood her parents' way of life, the defensive and sometimes bitter tone Nancy Reagan took about her relationships with her children in her 1989 memoir suggested that she was less understanding of her children's point of view.

The only exception to the pattern of on-again, off-again warmth between the Reagans and their children was their relationship with Ron Reagan Jr. — who was called Junior even by his parents despite the fact that his middle name is Prescott rather than his father's Wilson. Nancy Reagan has said that she is closer to Ron Jr. than any of the other three children, and both she and her husband seemed to accept his antics in good humor, though others thought they sometimes had cause to be embarrassed.

Ron Jr. had entered Yale at the age of eighteen, but he was unhappy there and dropped out after a few months to concentrate on becoming a professional dancer.

This seemed an impetuous step to many. He hadn't taken up dancing at all until his midteens, and it's highly unusual for anyone to succeed in this field unless they begin training before adolescence. To everyone's astonishment, he proved talented enough to win a job with the second company of the famed Joffrey Ballet and was later promoted to the senior company. While dancing with the Joffrey, Ron Jr. began living with his future wife, Doria. They were married at a City Hall ceremony in New York shortly after Ronald Reagan's November 1980 election to the presidency — easing Nancy Reagan's concerns about putting them up in the same room at the White House when they attended the inauguration in January. The supermarket tabloids had related rumors that Ron Jr. was gay and that the marriage was simply a union of convenience that wouldn't last a day longer than the Reagan presidency. But as of 1999 Ron Jr. and Doria were still married, although childless by choice.

Ron Jr. and Doria insisted on giving up their Secret Service protection in the first year of the Reagan presidency, although the press was never informed of the fact. In 1989, after his father's second term, Ron told *Newsday*, "It's hard to imagine what it's like being watched and followed by . . . guys carrying Uzis around all the time. Or to come back from a trip and find out they've been in your home and didn't really think to mention it to you. My wife and I decided we'd rather die than live like that."

Ron Jr. admitted that he and his father had disagreed on many subjects, from AIDS to the environment, from the homeless to abortion rights. "I'd see him talking to some right-to-lifers and I'd cringe. He's my father and I love him and he's entitled to his opinions, but I find [being against abortion rights] abhorrent." Ron sometimes felt that he was one of the few people who talked to his parents with full frankness. "There's a tremendous urge, especially in the White House, to be a rooting gallery and never voice any dissent. I just refused to go along with that. I don't think it does any good, least of all for the person who's President or First Lady. You've got to have some real feedback."

Such disagreements were largely private matters between himself and his parents — he was less likely to go public with any gripes he had than were Maureen, Michael, or Patti. But the Reagans were upset when he appeared in a TV documentary on safe sex in response to the growing AIDS epidemic, which came to the fore as a public health issue during his father's first term. The right wing tended to see AIDS as God's punishment for the "immoral" lives of gay men and drug users, the two groups most affected at the start, and President Reagan turned a deaf ear — in his case both proverbial and actual — to pleas for government action. Ron Jr.'s appearance on the program about AIDS thus created a considerable sensation in the press. But he has always maintained that he agreed to speak out because he thought it was extremely important, not just to embarrass his father into taking action. Eventually Ronald Reagan was persuaded that government funding to combat the disease was indeed necessary.

Ron Jr. also caused a considerable stir because of his penchant for taking off his pants in public, but this didn't seem to bother his parents at all. He was seen by millions in his underwear on television when he hosted *Saturday Night Live* and performed in a parody of the Tom Cruise star-making hit *Risky Business*. The supposed locale of this parody was changed from the suburban home of the movie to the White House, with Ron Jr. dancing around in a shirt, briefs, and socks. His father's reaction to this exposure was show business pride, expressed with a smiling, "Like father, like son." Nor were the Reagans aghast when he posed in tight red briefs for some *Vanity Fair* photographs by the famed photographer Annie Leibovitz. The Reagans, despite their current high position, had apparently not forgotten their Hollywood roots. Ronald Reagan, after all, had costarred with a chimp in *Bedtime for Bonzo* and had never felt the least need to apologize for doing so.

By the middle of his father's first term, Ron Jr. had given up his dancing career. Although he had come a long way quickly as a dancer, his late start was beginning to tell — he would clearly never achieve star rank, and there were more lucrative ways to earn a living, given the celebrity that went with being the President's son. He took up writing instead, and once again he had rapid success. It wasn't just his name — although that certainly helped. He demonstrated a genuine gift for humorous pieces and was soon published in a number of highly respectable publications, ranging from *Ladies' Home Journal* to *The Washington Post*. But he was most often published in *Playboy*, which paid as much as $10,000 an article. While it was hardly a publication on the approved list of Ronald Reagan's conservative supporters, there wasn't any great outcry about

Ron Jr.'s appearance in the magazine — perhaps because the pay was so impressive.

Ron Jr. then signed a three-year contract to provide a weekly feature for *Good Morning America*, starting in 1986. This upbeat feature was without a doubt the kind of endeavor that met with his parents' whole-hearted approval. Adding to their pleasure must have been the fact that Ron Jr. alone among their children resisted the chance to write a tell-all book. Patti's 1984 novel was followed by Michael's 1987 thrashing out of his problems in his own book, and even though Maureen waited until her father had left the White House, her 1989 *First Father, First Daughter* subjected the family to further dissection by the media. And while Nancy Reagan's own White House memoir allowed her to get her own licks in, its very title — *My Turn* — reveals its often combative nature. No White House family in history has ever told so many tales out of school, although the children of Franklin Delano Roosevelt came close in their later years, after their father's death. But Ron Jr. made it clear in several interviews that he couldn't understand telling so many stories about one's parents while they were still alive. He added that if his siblings were doing it for the family, "maybe they ought to be doing something else."

To judge by all of the books written by the children, and by Nancy herself, the Reagans were a troubled family before the White House entered the picture. As the columnist Maureen Dowd said in a 1989 review of Maureen Reagan's book in *The New Republic*, it was "about an American political family falling apart over and over and over" and that it seems remarkable "that Reagan was able to project so successfully the image of a genial patriarch working tirelessly in the cause of 'family values.'" She then added, "The White House is a distorting place." The degree to which it can magnify and bring into the open family troubles was never clearer than in the case of the Reagans.

13

∾

Lots of Grandchildren . . .
and an Only Child

George Herbert Walker Bush was the first sitting vice president in 150 years to be elected president in his own right without first succeeding to the presidency because of the incumbent's death, as had been the case with Theodore Roosevelt, Calvin Coolidge, Harry Truman, and Lyndon Johnson. The last president to achieve what Bush had was Martin Van Buren, in 1836. But Van Buren had been personally close to his predecessor, Andrew Jackson, and was well acquainted with the domestic workings of the White House. The Bushes were not. Although they had attended many state dinners during George Bush's eight years as vice president, the Reagans had invited them to dine privately with them only twice in that long period. After the 1988 election, though, Nancy Reagan did make a point of showing Barbara Bush every nook and cranny of the private quarters. This graciousness served two points. It quieted press stories about the lack of personal friendship between the Reagans and Bushes and served as a rebuke to Rosalynn Carter, who had given Nancy only a perfunctory tour of the White House after Reagan defeated Jimmy Carter in 1980.

As had been the case with the Reagans, all of the Bushes' children were fully grown.

They had four sons. The eldest, George, was not a Jr. Born in 1948, he was given the single middle name Walker. John (always called Jeb) was born in 1953. Neil Bush had been born in 1955, and the youngest son, Marvin, arrived a year later, in 1956. The Bushes also had a daughter, Dorothy (called "Doro"), born in 1959. Another daughter, Pauline, born in 1949, had died as a young child.

The Bush children were all married, and by the end of their father's single term as president, there were twelve Bush grand-children. The White House, Barbara Bush noted, could sleep twenty-eight comfortably, and sometimes it had to. President Bush said many times that it made him proud that all his children still came home to see their parents regularly — a comment that surely didn't endear him to the Reagans. But the most common gathering place for the clan was not the White House; the longtime Bush summer home in Kennebunkport, Maine, retained that honor. With so many grandchildren running around — the oldest (Jeb's son George) only twelve at the start, and five of them four or younger — the press had great difficulty in telling them apart and largely gave up on the task of captioning photographs with their actual names. Thus none of the grandchildren became the focus of any particular attention or public interest.

Even the Bush sons and daughter drew headlines only occasionally. The only one to become embroiled in controversy was Neil, who had been a director of the Denver thrift institution that would become a centerpiece of the savings-and-loan scandal of the early 1990s. He had been on the board of Silverado Banking, Savings, and Loan only for three years, from 1985–1988, but when it went belly-up like so many other institutions, his name kept appearing in articles noting that the nationwide banking mess could cost the taxpayers hundreds of billions of dollars. It was ironic that he should be the Bush son in trouble. President Bush had said that Neil was the one child who could be called perfect, and in fact his brothers and sisters sometimes teased him by calling him "Mr. Perfect." Neil maintained that he had done absolutely nothing wrong and was being singled out simply because he was the President's son. In the end he was absolved of wrongdoing. It became evident that he had been put on the board largely because his father was vice president at the time. His case illustrated the perils of being the son or daughter of a vice president or president.

While his father was president, son George became the managing partner of the Texas Rangers baseball team after putting together a group of investors to buy it. That association was more likely to get him mentioned on the sports pages than in any political reportage. Jeb, who was secretary of commerce for the state of Florida, and Marvin, a financial consultant, were almost never in the national news. It was not until 1994 that son George ran for governor of Texas and won, while Jeb lost his race for governor of Florida. In 1998 George won reelection as governor of Texas, and Jeb ran again and won the governorship of Florida. Following in his father's footsteps, George was already the front-runner for the Republican presidential nomination in the year 2000.

In 1992 daughter Doro was in the news because she was getting married. But while Tricia Nixon and both Johnson daughters had had weddings that received massive television and print coverage, the Bushes presided over a family wedding that took place under the cover of a virtual news blackout. That was because the marriage of Doro to Robert Koch was a second one. She had previously been married to William LeBlond, and the couple had two children, Sam, 7, and Ellie, 5, who acted as attendants at their mother's ceremony on Saturday, June 27, 1992.

The wedding, witnessed by about 130 guests, was a very private affair that took place at Camp David, the presidential retreat in the Maryland mountains. Even such close political allies to George Bush as Vice President Dan Quayle and Secretary of State James A. Baker III "apparently did not make the guest list," according to the *Los Angeles Times*, which noted that "the White House has tried mightily to keep all details under wraps, but some have leaked out." The absence of the Vice President and other top Republican figures was in keeping with the "non-political" nature of the occasion

— necessitated by the fact that the groom had been a top aide to Democratic House Majority Leader Richard A. Gephardt, who had been invited because of that connection but had to decline because of a fund-raiser in his home state of Missouri. Groom Bobby Koch had left his job as an aide to Gephardt two weeks earlier to take a new position with the Washington office of the Wine Institute, thus avoiding a direct political conflict of interest within the Bush family.

All in all, the Bush children had far less impact on public consciousness than most presidential children, whether youngsters or adults. Barbara Bush's dog, Millie, became far better known to the public, thanks to the best-selling book about her life at the White House. But with both George and Jeb Bush building major political reputations, the press is bound to be speculating for years to come about the possibility of there being another set of White House kids named Bush sometime in the twenty-first century.

The public had admired the Bushes as a collective family, but in 1992 the possibility that there would be a young child in the White House excited a good deal of curiosity, as was widely reflected in the press.

Chelsea Victoria Clinton, born February 27, 1980, was three and a half years older than Amy Carter had been when she moved into the White House, and she'd already had to deal with rougher political waters than Amy had. Her father, William Jefferson Clinton — who, like Jimmy Carter, opted for the informal and styled himself simply Bill Clinton — was serving his fourth term as governor of Arkansas at the time of his 1992 election as president.

Arkansas politics have always been rough, and Chelsea was exposed to numerous unpleasant charges and innuendos against her father over the years of her childhood. Bill and Hillary Clinton had had a long, serious talk with her about how to cope with these pressures when Chelsea was only nine. Thus, in some ways, Chelsea was prepared for the glass-house aspects of living in the White House.

But the Clintons, mindful of the cruel jokes that had been made about Amy Carter's looks and activities when she was the first daughter, were determined to protect Chelsea during the White House years. Despite their own high profile during the 1980s, the Clintons had paid a great deal of attention to their daughter. One or the other of them had read to her every night until she preferred to read by herself, and it was Governor Bill Clinton who drove her to public school every morning. Giving a commencement address at her alma mater, Wellesley College, in May 1992, Hillary Rodham Clinton had said, "I remember one very long night when my daughter, Chelsea, was about four weeks old and crying inconsolably. Nothing from my political science major seemed to help at all. Finally, I looked at her in my arms, and I said, 'Chelsea, you've never been a baby before, and I've never been a mother before. We are just going to have to help each other get through this together.' And so far, we have. And for Bill and me, she has been the great joy of our life, and watching her grow and flourish has given greater urgency to the task of helping all children."

Because Bill Clinton had emphasized the issue of education both as governor of Arkansas and during the presidential campaign, it would have been politically wise to send Chelsea to public school, as the Carters had decided to do in Amy's case. But they were very worried about protecting their daughter from the press, and a public school seemed to offer far less control in that respect. In the end they sent her to the Sidwell Friends School, a private Quaker institution founded in 1883 where a number of politicians' daughters, including Julie and Tricia Nixon, had gone.

The Clintons managed to spoon-feed the press what they wanted the public to know about Chelsea. A typical example, published right after the 1992 election in *The Atlanta Journal and Constitution*, read as follows:

> *Chelsea Clinton, 12, was named for the Judy Collins song "Chelsea Morning." When she grows up, she wants to be an astronautical engineer and even journey into space someday. Chelsea takes ballet lessons, plays volleyball and softball, and likes to read. What she really wants right now is to get her ears pierced.*

No interviews with Chelsea were allowed, and given the predigested nature of the information being released by her parents, other sources were turned to for adding a little spice to stories about the incoming first daughter. *The New York Times* managed to get the Reagans' controversial daughter Patti Davis to dispense some advice. Because little food was kept in the upstairs kitchen in the White House family quarters, Patti suggested that Chelsea get her own refrigerator. "Unless you like late-night snacks of mayonnaise and salad dressing, I'd advise keeping your room well-stocked." On the problem of having constant security surveillance, she said, "Ask your Secret Service guards to lose the dark suits and try something casual, such as L.L. Bean. And don't try to shake them; you'll just make them mad." Patti also noted the importance of the White House secret passageways as places to hide out: "If you can't find them, call me or ask the maids." A suggestion that Chelsea "get some music going in that place" seemed unnecessary, given Bill Clinton's penchant for public saxophone playing. Most important, Patti said, "Dress however you want, wear your hair however you want, say what you think, don't be afraid to make mistakes, and don't forget to laugh."

How much of this advice was actually taken is difficult to say. Although Chelsea always appeared poised in public and was often photographed in the company of her parents, there were many ways in which she led the most sheltered White House life of any presidential child since the Cleveland children a century earlier. Her parents occasionally gave out a few tidbits of information, as when Hillary revealed that Chelsea and some visiting friends had been told to clean up the White House movie theater themselves after they scattered popcorn all over it. The public was allowed to know a lot about Chelsea's relationship with her cat, Socks, but not a great deal else. She did appear, along with many other Washington children, in an annual Christmas production of the ballet *The Nutcracker* at the Kennedy Center, and pictures of her onstage were widely published. But, as usual, there were no interviews and no personal stories about the experience made available.

In some ways it's surprising that the press allowed the Clintons to get away with this successful attempt to keep Chelsea's life under wraps. But perhaps the plethora of negative stories about both Bill and Hillary Clinton during a very aggressive era of press coverage served to insulate Chelsea to a degree. The Johnson daughters and Amy Carter had been subjected to very nasty stories about their looks, and perhaps the press had grown squeamish about attacking White House children. One tabloid did focus on Chelsea's looks, but with a twist: They used a computer projection to show that she would turn into a "beauty" by the time she was eighteen!

During her father's reelection campaign against Senator Robert Dole in 1996,

Chelsea made some appearances with her parents, but as in 1992 she did no campaigning as such. At her father's second inauguration, she joined her parents in walking down Pennsylvania Avenue and waving to the crowds. The *Los Angeles Times* wrote, "She appeared confident and attractive, wearing a stylish suit with a miniskirt." Perhaps as a rebuke to Hillary Clinton, Mr. Blackwell's best-dressed list for 1996 had included Chelsea as one of its "fabulous fashion independents."

In March of 1997, Chelsea accompanied her mother on a trip to Africa. In the village of Arusha, Tanzania, her mother astonished the media by suggesting that Chelsea might like to answer some questions from teenagers in the crowd. Asked about the problems facing young people in America, she confidently answered, "We have a big problem with drugs and people not thinking they have a future. There is a lot of hopelessness." Then, "sounding like a chip off her parents' block," as the *Los Angeles Times* put it, she said that the answer to such problems "has to come from the young people themselves. I think that's something we have to work on. We've got to realize that we are the future." When these comments appeared on American news programs, it marked the first time that the public had ever heard Chelsea Clinton's voice. Yet it sounded as though she had been making speeches for years.

In the fall of 1997, Chelsea entered college. Although she still didn't give any interviews, the press covered the event as major news. Back in May when she had announced her choice as California's Stanford University, the *Arizona Republic* carried a typical piece on the subject. "Stanford University is a prestigious choice, to be sure. But in selecting the West Coast school, Chelsea rejected the likes of Harvard, Princeton, and Brown, along with her parents' alma maters — Georgetown University, a few measly miles from the White House, and Wellesley, just up the Eastern seaboard. She also turned her back on Yale University, where her parents met in law school."

President Clinton said of the decision, "She had wonderful choices, and she made her own decision, and her mother and I are proud of her, and we support her. She didn't have a bad choice. She just picked the decision she thought was best for her." The press, as might be expected, kept reminding everyone that she had picked a college that was just about as far away from the White

House as possible. But they were probably making too much of that. The President had gone to California more often than any other state during his presidency, and during Chelsea's first year of college, he and Hillary visited her several times. She was also home for all of her vacations and was reportedly in constant telephone touch with her parents. In the spring of 1998 it was even reported that the Clintons had met the parents of her new boyfriend, and both sets of parents dutifully sang the praises of the other's child.

When Chelsea started college, *Harper's Bazaar* carried a new article by Patti Davis, titled "Chelsea and Me." In it Patti harked back to when her father had first been elected governor of California, in 1966. She recalled wailing, "How could you do this to me?" and commented that "in the photographs of my father's swearing-in, I look like someone has just cut my thumb off and fed it to me." She went on to write that she had watched Chelsea Clinton throughout the 1993 inauguration week, looking "for signs of angst and inner turmoil, but instead I saw a serenity that fascinated me."

Patti commended Chelsea for the "poise and dignity" she had shown throughout her first five White House years, adding, "I wish

I had possessed those qualities when my father was president." Patti does not regret the opinions she expressed that were in opposition to her father but says, "I ache over the way I expressed them." It is ironic that a former White House daughter, who was called upon to offer advice to Chelsea when she took up residence in the President's House, should now find Chelsea to be a personal "inspiration."

It has almost always happened that former presidents, no matter how much they may have been at political odds in their years in office, develop a new rapport after they leave the White House. By then they have become fellow members of what has been called "the world's most exclusive club." For former White House kids there is also a degree of shared experience that leads to a subtle emotional link. Some former White House kids choose to fade as much as possible from public view, but those who gather for the occasional conference at a college campus or agree to be interviewed on television in small groups have much to share among themselves. The presidents who were their fathers may have been very different from one another, but the glass jail on Pennsylvania Avenue gives them, inevitably, a view of the world that creates an almost subliminal bond. Their children also have seen the world from a unique vantage point and can't help but empathize to some degree with one another's experiences. Some, like Jesse Grant, may remember the White House as "the best playground in the world," a view more common among those who were quite young when their fathers were president. Others, like the Nixon or Johnson daughters — whose memories of the White House are bound to be haunted by the echo of protestors screaming imprecations outside the White House fence — must have decidedly mixed feelings. But it seems unlikely that any of them would have passed up the chance to be a White House kid, to live in the President's House, to spend a few years at the center of American life, to know the heartbeat of their country in a way that few are privileged to do.

Presidential Families

This chronology of presidential families includes all the children of American presidents who survived to the time of their father's election. A number of children of presidents, especially in the nineteenth century, died at an early age. Many of the children listed here were adults when their fathers became president and only visited the White House rather than lived in it on a regular basis, as is noted throughout the text of this book. Some grandchildren also lived in the White House, and while they are not listed here, their stories are included in the narrative. The dates given are for the term(s) of office.

1789–1797   Washington, George and Martha Dandridge Custis
Jacky, Little Patt (These were the children of Martha Custis from her first marriage. The Washingtons were the only presidential family who never lived in the White House, which was not completed until

the end of the John Adams administration.)

1797–1801 Adams, John and Abigail Smith
Abigail, John, Charles, Thomas

1801–1809 Jefferson, Thomas and Martha Wayles Skelton
Martha, Maria (Martha Jefferson died before her husband was elected president.)

1809–1817 Madison, James and Dolley Payne Todd
Payne Todd (Payne was Dolley Madison's son by her first husband.)

1817–1825 Monroe, James and Elizabeth Kortright
Eliza, Maria

1825–1829 Adams, John Quincy and Louisa Catherine Johnson
George, John, Charles

1829–1837 Jackson, Andrew and Rachel Donelson Robards
Andrew Jackson Jr. (Rachel Jackson died just after her husband's election. Andrew Jr. was an adopted child.)

1837–1841 Van Buren, Martin and Hannah Hoes
Abraham, John, Martin, Smith

1841	Harrison, William Henry and Anna Symmes Elizabeth, John Cleves, Lucy, William Henry Jr., John Scott, Benjamin, Mary, Carter, Ann (President Harrison died within a month of his inauguration.)
1841–1845	Tyler, John and Letitia Christian; Julia Gardner Mary, Robert, John Jr., Letitia, Elizabeth, Alice, Tazewell (The first Mrs. Tyler died while her husband was president. He married Julia Gardner later in his term, and they had another seven children after he left office.)
1845–1849	Polk, James Knox and Sarah Childress (The Polks had no children.)
1849–1850	Taylor, Zachary and Margaret Smith Anne, Mary Elizabeth, Richard (Zachary Taylor died in office.)
1850–1853	Fillmore, Millard and Abigail Powers Abigail, Powers
1853–1857	Pierce, Franklin and Jane Means Appleton

Benjamin (Benjamin was killed in a train accident after his father's election but before his inauguration.)

1857–1861   Buchanan, James
(James Buchanan was the only bachelor president.)

1861–1865   Lincoln, Abraham and Mary Todd
Robert, Edward, William, Thomas (President Lincoln was assassinated a month after the beginning of his second term.)

1865–1869   Johnson, Andrew and Eliza McCardle
Robert, Martha, Mary, Andrew Jr.

1869–1877   Grant, Ulysses Simpson and Julia Dent
Frederick, Ulysses Simpson Jr., Ellen, Jesse

1877–1881   Hayes, Rutherford Birchard and Lucy Webb
Birchard, Webb, Rutherford, Fanny, Scott

1881   Garfield, James Abram and Lucretia Rudolph
Harry, James, Mollie, Irvin, Abram (President Garfield

was shot by an assassin in July of his first year in office and died in September.)

1881–1885	Arthur, Chester Alan and Ellen Lewis Herndon Chester Alan Jr., Ellen
1885–1889	Cleveland, Grover and Frances Folsom Ruth, Esther, Marion, Richard, Francis (Grover Cleveland was a bachelor when elected and married during his term of office.)
1889–1893	Harrison, Benjamin and Caroline Scott Russell, Mary Scott, Elizabeth
1893–1897	Cleveland, Grover and Francis Folsom (see 1885)
1897–1901	McKinley, William and Ida Saxton (The McKinleys' two daughters died at a young age. President McKinley was assassinated early in his second term.)
1901–1909	Roosevelt, Theodore and Alice H. Lee; Edith Kermit Carow Alice, Theodore Jr., Kermit, Ethel, Archibald, Quentin (Roosevelt's first wife died soon after the birth of her daughter Alice.)

1909–1913	Taft, William Howard and Helen Herron
	Robert, Helen, Charles
1913–1921	Wilson, Woodrow and Ellen Axson; Edith Bolling Galt
	Margaret, Jessie, Eleanor (The first Mrs. Wilson died during her husband's first term; he then married Mrs. Galt, herself a widow.)
1921–1923	Harding, Warren Gamiel and Florence Kling DeWolfe
	(The Hardings had no children, and he died in office.)
1923–1929	Coolidge, Calvin and Grace Ann Goodhue
	John, Calvin Jr.
1929–1933	Hoover, Herbert Clark and Lou Henry
	Herbert Jr., Allan Henry
1933–1945	Roosevelt, Franklin Delano and Anna Eleanor
	James, Anna, Elliott, Franklin Jr., John (President Roosevelt died in office early in his fourth term.)
1945–1953	Truman, Harry S. and Elizabeth Wallace
	Margaret
1953–1961	Eisenhower, Dwight David

and Mamie Geneva Doud
John Sheldon Doud

1961–1963   Kennedy, John Fitzgerald and Jacqueline Lee Bouvier
Caroline, John Jr. (President Kennedy was assassinated in November 1963.)

1963–1969   Johnson, Lyndon Baines and Claudia (Lady Bird) Taylor
Luci Baines, Lynda Bird

1969–1974   Nixon, Richard Milhous and Thelma Patricia Ryan
Tricia, Julie (President Nixon resigned from office in August 1974.)

1974–1977   Ford, Gerald Rudolph and Elizabeth Boomer Warren
Michael, Jack, Steve, Susan

1977–1981   Carter, James Earl and Rosalynn Smith
James Earl III, John Williams, Donnel Jeffrey, Amy

1981–1989   Reagan, Ronald Wilson and Jane Wyman; Nancy Davis
Maureen, Michael, Patti Davis, Ronald Jr. (Maureen is Reagan's daughter with Jane Wyman, and Michael was adopted by them; Nancy Reagan is the mother of Patti and Ron Jr.)

1989–1993	Bush, George Herbert Walker and Barbara Pierce
	George, Jeb, Neil, Marvin, Dorothy
1993–(2001)	Clinton, William Jefferson and Hillary Rodham
	Chelsea

Bibliography

Barnard, Harry. *Rutherford B. Hayes and His America.* Indianapolis: Bobbs-Merrill, 1954.

Blue, Rose, and Corinne J. Nader. *The White House Kids.* (Juvenile). Brookfield, Conn.: Milbrook Press, 1995.

Bush, Barbara. *Barbara Bush, A Memoir.* New York: Lisa Drew/Scribners, 1994.

Caroli, Betty Boyd. *Inside the White House.* New York: Canopy Books, 1992.

Carter, Rosalynn. *First Lady from Plains.* Boston: Houghton Mifflin, 1984.

Eisenhower, Julie Nixon. *Pat Nixon: The Untold Story.* New York: Simon & Schuster, 1986.

Eisenhower, Susan. *Mrs. Ike.* New York: Farrar, Straus, and Giroux, 1996.

Farley, James A. *Jim Farley's Story, The Roosevelt Years.* New York: McGraw Hill, 1948.

Ferrell, Robert H. *Truman, A Centenary Remembrance.* New York: Viking, 1984.

Ford, Betty, with Chris Chase. *The Times of My Life.* New York: Harper & Row/Reader's Digest, 1978.

Johnson, Lady Bird. *A White House Diary.* New York: Holt, Rinehart, and Winston, 1970.

King, Norman. *The Woman in the White House.* New York: Birch Lane, 1996.

McFeely, William S. *Grant.* New York: Norton, 1981.

Malone, Dumas, and Basil Rauch. *Empire for Liberty,* Vols. I and II. New York: Appleton, Century Crofts, 1960.

Malone, John. *The Civil War Quiz Book.* New York: Quill/Morrow, 1992.

Manchester, William. *The Glory and the Dream,* Vols. I and II. Boston: Little, Brown, 1974.

Mayo, Edith P., gen. ed. *The Smithsonian Book of the First Ladies.* New York: Holt, 1996.

O'Donnell, Kenneth P., and David Powers, with Joe McCarthy. *"Johnny, We Hardly Knew Ye."* Boston: Little, Brown, 1972.

Parks, Lillian Rogers. *My Thirty Years Backstairs at the White House.* New York: Fleet, 1961.

Randall, Ruth Painter. *Mary Lincoln, The Biography of a Marriage.* Boston: Little, Brown, 1953.

Reagan, Nancy, with William Novak. *My Turn.* New York: Random House, 1989.

Roosevelt, Eleanor. *This I Remember.* New York: Harper, 1949.

Ross, Ishbel. *Grace Coolidge and Her Era.* New York: Dodd Mead, 1962.

Seale, William. *The President's House.* Washington, D.C.: White House Historical Association/National Geographic/Harry Abrams, 1986.

Smith, Gene. *High Crimes and Misdemeanors, The Impeachment and Trial of Andrew Johnson.* New York: Morrow, 1977.

Smith, Merriman. *A White House Memoir.* New York: Norton, 1972.

Teague, Michael. *Mrs. L, Conversations with Alice Roosevelt Longworth.* New York: Doubleday, 1981.

Teichmann, Howard. *Alice, The Life and Times of Alice Roosevelt Longworth.* Englewood Cliffs, N.J.: Prentice Hall, 1979.

Truman, Margaret. *Harry S. Truman.* New York: Morrow, 1973.

Welch, Richard E. Jr. *The Presidencies of Grover Cleveland.* Lawrence, Kans.: The University Press of Kansas, 1988.